CONTENTS

Selected Glossary		iii
I.	THE PROBLEM	1
II.	STRATEGIC TRIADS: RATIONALES AND HISTORY	2
III.	DOCTRINE	4
IV.	STRATEGIC POSTURE: THE RANGE OF CHOICE	8
	Move to a Dyad	9
	Leave Silo-housed ICBM in Place	11
	Phase Out Silo-housed ICBM	18
	Strategic Choice: Images of Power and Deterrent Effect	26
V.	SOME ARMS-CONTROL CONSIDERATIONS	28
VI.	CONCLUSION	30
Appendix I: Strategic Missiles		32
Appendix II: Strategic Bombers		36

SELECTED GLOSSARY

A<small>IRS</small> (Advanced Inertial Reference Sphere). A new guidance system consisting of a 10·3-inch diameter sphere containing a cluster of inertial navigation instruments floating without gimbals in a neutrally buoyant state in a highly controlled thermal environment. Designed to reduce the gyroscopic drift which decreases missile accuracy. Scheduled for deployment on board the MX ICBM.

Assured destruction. The ability to inflict on an adversary a degree of punishment believed to be certain to be unacceptable.

A<small>WACS</small> (Airborne Warning and Control System). A system comprising a 'look-down' radar and flying command post for directing manned interceptors.

C<small>EP</small> (circular error probable). The measure of missile accuracy: estimated radius of a circle within which 50 per cent of re-entry vehicles are expected to land.

Cold launch. Technique for ejecting a missile from silo or submarine launch tube by low-pressure gas. First-stage rocket motors ignite once the missile clears the silo or water surface. Enables the usable diameter of an ICBM silo to be increased by up to 50 per cent (because internal shielding can be removed, and little space is required for the escape of exhaust gases); also, silos may be 'reloaded' (cold launching causes little damage to them), and silo aperture can be greatly reduced (exhaust gases are minimal), thereby increasing 'hardness'.

Collateral damage. Damage inflicted as a secondary effect of military action.

Counter-force. Military action applied directly against military forces.

Counter-value. Military action applied directly against civilian-economic 'assets'.

Cross-targeting. Attack-planning tactic of assigning a target to warheads carried by different delivery vehicles.

Cruise missile. A pilotless air-breathing vehicle powered continuously during its flight.

Damage limitation. A strategy which seeks to deny an adversary access to civilian-economic targets.

Depressed trajectory. Trajectory of a ballistic missile fired at a much lower angle than the normal minimum-energy trajectory. Firing on depressed trajectory, by reducing both the warning time line-of-sight radars can provide and the missile's flight time, pose major threats to forces that depend on warning time for their security (alert bombers or, hypothetically, dash-mobile ICBM systems).

Dyad. A strategic force structure that has two 'legs' (most probably submarines and bombers).

E<small>MP</small> (electromagnetic pulse). A nuclear-weapon effect (the creation of electrical and magnetic fields) which can destroy or impair the performance of electronic equipment and wipe clean computer memories.

E<small>MT</small> (equivalent megatonnage). A measure of the surface damage (by blast) that a nuclear force could inflict, expressed in terms of 'one megaton equivalents'. Damage from a nuclear explosion diminishes from the point on the earth's surface closest to the explosion as a function of the cube root of the yield of the warhead. $E_{MT} = NY^{2/3}$, where N is the number of warheads, and Y their yields.

F<small>BS</small> (forward-based systems). American nuclear-capable aircraft and missiles deployed in and around Europe (and North-East Asia) that have the range to attack the Soviet Union.

F<small>OBS</small> (Fractional-orbital bombardment systems). A ballistic missile that achieves orbital velocity but fires retro-rockets for re-entry before one orbit of the earth is completed.

Fratricide. The phenomenon whereby nuclear warhead explosions create such turbulent local conditions that other incoming warheads are damaged, destroyed or made to deviate from their intended trajectories.

Hard-target counter-force. A strategic doctrine and capabilities designed to destroy hard military targets (i.e., missile silos and command-and-control facilities).

Inertial guidance. The basic guidance system for ballistic missiles, capable of detecting and correcting for deviation from intended trajectory or velocity.

L<small>OW</small>/LTA (launch on warning/launch through attack). Firing tactics for fixed-site weapon systems that cannot ride out an attack. L<small>OW</small> means firing on receipt of radar warning from satellite and ground-based early-warning systems. L<small>TA</small> would involve delaying firing until some warheads had arrived (precluding the possibility of launch on false warning).

L<small>SO</small> (limited strategic options). Very discriminating nuclear targeting options – at the low and very low end of the scale of possible punishment. Usually contrasted sharply with massive attacks – despite the fact that the scale of damage, in theory if not in terms of pre-planned options, is a continuum.

M<small>ARV</small> (manoeuvring re-entry vehicle). An RV (which may or may not be powered) that manoeuvres in order to improve accuracy or evade ABM defences.

M<small>IRV</small> (multiple independently-targetable re-entry vehicle). An RV containing several warhead packages, each of which may be directed to a separate target. American MIRV systems currently are deployed on *Minutemen* III (ICBM) and *Poseidon* (SLBM); Soviet systems are on SS-17, SS-18 Mod 2 and SS-19 (ICBM), and SS-20 (IRBM).

MX The follow-on ICBM system which the United States may deploy to replace *Minuteman* II and III and *Titan* II. MX is being designed with a view to deployment in land-mobile modes.

N<small>AVSTAR</small> (navigation system using time and ranging). A Global Positioning System comprising 24 satellites to be 'parked' in synchronous orbits (i.e. at orbital speeds identical to that of the earth's rotation), designed to provide near-continuous signals which may be monitored by passive receivers on board ICBM (for example). Four such signals, plus orbital details from satellites, will enable a missile to determine its position to within 20–30ft and so correct its attitude or velocity.

P<small>BV</small> (post-boost vehicle). Permits a missile to make late-course powered corrections in trajectory for improved accuracy. Generally (though not invariably) associated with a MIRV option.

Precision guidance. A family of technologies, still in an early stage of development, that permits an attacking vehicle to home on its target by recognizing some dis-

iii

tinctive signature given off by, or associated with, that target.

Preferential defence. Selective coverage of a missile field in order to defend some silos rather than others. An attacker could not know in advance which silos would be defended and in what strength.

Psi overpressure. Transient pressure (in pounds per square inch) above normal atmospheric pressure. The measure commonly used to determine an object's ability to withstand the pressure from a nuclear blast.

SIOP (Single integrated Operational Plan). The strategic nuclear war plan of the United States.

Stability. Arms Race Stability is a condition in which neither side is strongly motivated greatly to 'improve' existing weapon systems, introduce new ones, or increase existing quantitative force goals. Crisis Stability is a condition in which neither side is seriously tempted to launch a first strike, the 'first-strike bonus' being judged of trivial worth. Weapon System Stability is a condition in which only those weapon systems that are deemed (tautologically) to be stabilizing are deployed. Definitions of stability tend to betray the political preferences and doctrinal assumptions of their authors.

Throw-weight (of missile). The total weight of the re-entry vehicle(s) plus guidance unit which can be delivered over a particular range and in a stated trajectory.

Triad. A strategic force structure that has three 'legs': hitherto ICBM, submarines and manned bombers.

War fighting. A doctrine and a force structure designed primarily to engage an adversary's military forces (and their essential support) directly, rather than to punish him by threatening/striking his civilian-economic assets. Soviet war-fighting doctrine is often contrasted, falsely, with American *deterrent* doctrine. It should be contrasted with the assured destruction doctrine: each is designed to produce deterrent effect.

Yield. The force of a nuclear explosion expressed in terms of tons of TNT that would produce the same explosive energy. Nuclear warhead yields are expressed in kilotons, or KT (thousands of tons of TNT), and megatons or MT (millions of tons of TNT).

The Future of Land-Based Missile Forces

I. THE PROBLEM

This Paper addresses what must become 'the question of the decade' in the 1980s for both super-powers with respect to their strategic policies: what is to be done about fixed-site, land-based missile forces? Weapon-system components are now being developed, and indeed deployed, which will radically transform the cost-attack ratio of hard-target counter-force strikes.[1] By the mid- to late 1980s, on current projections, neither super-power will be able to retain sufficient confidence in the ability of its fixed-site intercontinental ballistic missile (ICBM) force to ride out a surprise attack and remain a secure second-strike instrument.

There will be no precise dates in the 1980s when each super-power will be able to judge that this has happened – though American officials most frequently refer to about 1984 as the likely year[2] – and much of the present debate on strategic forces is focused upon competing threat assessments for particular periods. In the heat of this debate, however, with its exchange of detailed quantitative analyses,[3] it is easy to lose sight of the fact that both super-powers are approaching major and unprecedented decision points concerning the structure of their strategic forces.

The problem that the predictable vulnerability of silo-housed ICBM will set the super-powers defies simple statement. It will be posed differently in each country and cannot sensibly be reduced to a series of comparative cost-effectiveness studies designed to indicate which system, or mix of systems, should replace fixed-site ICBM forces. However, the block obsolescence (for some important purposes) of an entire 'leg' of the strategic triad will be an event so momentous that its anticipation should be the occasion for a fundamental review of strategic doctrine. Therefore, although the problem in the 1980s may be identified as the growing theoretical vulnerability of missile silos, doctrinal assumptions are bound to influence the analysis of alternative solutions. Neither super-power is likely to be able to effect a totally disarming first strike, regardless of the theoretical vulnerability or otherwise of ICBM silos and bombers on runways, but perceptions of particular asymmetries in strategic capability could have a very negative impact upon both pre- and intra-war deterrence.

Prognosis of the vulnerability and capabilities of the other two legs of the strategic triad are critically important to an assessment of the future of land-based missile forces. The 1980s should see no well-founded cause for alarm about the survivability of nuclear-powered ballistic-missile

---

[1] For a brief summary see *Strategic Survey 1974* (London: IISS, 1975), pp. 46–50; for specific detail see Appendices I and II below. Hard targets are missile silos, their launch-control centres (LCC), and some other command-and-control facilities. Hard targets may also be of a civilian character – for example, dams.

[2] In mid-1977 the American defence community appears to have reached at least a temporary consensus on the proposition that the *Minuteman/Titan* force will be unacceptably vulnerable for second-strike duties in 1984, give or take a year. Even if 1986–88 is a better guess, the problem remains.

[3] Useful examples include: Paul H. Nitze, 'Deterring our Deterrent', *Foreign Policy*, No. 25 (Winter 1976–7), pp. 195–210; Edward N. Luttwak, *Strategic Power: Military Capabilities and Political Utility*, (Part III), The Washington Papers, Vol. IV, No. 38 (Beverly Hills, Cal.: Center for Strategic and International Studies, 1976); and Thomas J. Downey, 'How To Avoid Monad – And Disaster', *Foreign Policy*, No. 24 (Fall 1976), pp. 172–201. A view strongly sceptical of the proposition that ICBM silos face short- to medium-term vulnerability problems can be found in John D. Steinbruner and Thomas M. Garwin, 'Strategic Vulnerability: The Balance Between Prudence and Paranoia', *International Security*, Vol. 1, No. 1 (Summer 1976), pp. 138–81.

submarines (SSBN) and manned bombers. Nevertheless, despite generation changes in SSBN, submarine-launched ballistic missile (SLBM) and manned bomber technologies, these 'legs' of the triad are very imperfect substitutes for a land-based missile force that is charged with more than an assured destruction mission. SSBN are far from ideal recipients of lengthy and complex targeting/firing instructions,[4] and manned or unmanned bombers could take eight hours to reach their weapon-release points. If it is decided that the strategic forces must be capable of flexible employment – including the destruction of very limited target systems and the prompt neutralization of some of the adversary's reserve silo-housed (or re-loadable) ICBM withheld from the first strike, or of other enemy resources such as active defences – the required weapon-system performance characteristics would be very difficult, if not impossible, to meet with SSBN, manned bombers or cruise missiles. The strategic forces must include weapons which lend themselves to very reliable command and control, which are extremely accurate, swift in mission accomplishment, and able to survive an attempted disarming strike. For the mid-1980s and beyond, the silo-housed ICBM satisfies all conditions save the last. In these circumstances, what should be the strategic-policy response of the super-powers to the predictable condition of vulnerable ICBM silos?

II. STRATEGIC TRIADS: RATIONALES AND HISTORY

By the time that Robert McNamara conducted his review of targeting plans and required strategic forces in 1961 (the 'Hickey study'), the triadic structure was a foregone conclusion.

He inherited a B-47/B-52/B-58 bomber force to which the Air Force was profoundly attached, a land-based ICBM programme which was about to produce a missile capable of in-silo launch (*Minuteman* I), and a *Polaris* SLBM programme which had attained an initial operating capability (with two boats) in 1960. Given that the Kennedy Administration was ushered into office partly as a result of alarm about the state of American defences, given also the counterforce preferences of McNamara's principal advisers (a range of targeting strategies requiring more, rather than fewer, warheads) and the tremendous organizational momentum behind the major weapon programmes, it is scarcely surprising that the United States adopted a triad.

The later models of the B-52 were retained, but in order to ward off Air Force demands for a follow-on long-range bomber (initially the B-70) McNamara had to stress the continued viability of the B-52, and to offer a very large procurement of ICBM in compensation. In addition, the *Polaris* system functioned so well, and was so perfectly attuned to the official emphasis on survivability, that McNamara expanded (and accelerated) the programme to 41 boats (four fewer than the Navy wanted, but probably twelve more than the Eisenhower Administration would have funded).[5]

There is much to recommend Michael Howard's dictum that: 'It is not in the nature of great powers to acquiesce in the monopoly by their rivals of a major military weapon, if they are in a position to acquire it themselves'.[6] The Soviet Long-Range Air Force clearly illustrated this point with the unveiling of the Mya-4 *Bison* and the Tu-95 *Bear* in 1954–55, though it could not compete with the vast American numerical lead in strategic bombers – in the mid-1950s, the Strategic Air Command (SAC) inventory included a total of 1,485 B-47. Similarly, the Soviet Union's deployment of first-generation ICBM in 1959 meant that the United States would have to follow suit, whether or not the manned bomber fleet was held to be substantially at risk as a consequence. Soviet emulation of the *Polaris*

---

[4] Very low frequency (VLF) communications can be jammed, destroyed or interdicted by 'natural' environmental phenomena. Extremely low frequency (ELF) communications have a very restricted traffic-bearing capacity. See Desmond J. Ball, 'Déja Vu: The Return of Counterforce in the Nixon Administration (Or, The Politics of Potential Nuclear Castration)', in Robert O'Neill, ed., *The Strategic Nuclear Balance: An Australian Perspective* (Canberra: Strategic and Defence Studies Centre, Australian National University, 1974), pp. 211–12.

[5] In January 1961, McNamara inherited specific authorization for 19 *Polaris* submarines and 450 *Minuteman* ICBM (in addition to 250 *Atlas* and *Titan* ICBM).
[6] Michael Howard, *Studies in War and Peace* (London: Temple Smith, 1970), p. 149.

programme came nine years later with the deployment of the *Yankee*-class SSBN in 1969, fitted with the 1,520nm-range SS-N-6 SLBM. (Until 1969, Soviet SLBM and sea-launched cruise missiles (SLCM) had all been short-range.)

Though the strategic triad has existed only since 1959–60, a tripartite structure has become widely accepted as natural and inevitable. It is easy to criticize the United States' strategic triad as developed in the 1960s on the grounds that it provided needless overinsurance. Some prescient analysts saw that silo-housed ICBM would inevitably become vulnerable, but in 1961–62 such a situation – affecting the 1970s or beyond – seemed distant, or was not believed at all. However, for a mission so vital as strategic deterrence it was not unreasonable to avoid depending upon a single set of technologies, and, moreover, the Soviet Union might have succeeded in deploying a moderately competent, thick urban area anti-ballistic missile (ABM) defence system. Therefore, as a means of deepening the problems facing Soviet defence planners (particularly that of attack timing) and of providing more warheads with extended target coverage (and to saturate any ABM defences), and also as a general safeguard, a major programme of SLBM deployment was prudent. But was it necessary to retain a long-range bomber force with a strength of 500–600?[7]

On strategic grounds there was no shortage of answers to this. Bombers, unlike ICBM and SLBM, can be launched, set in a holding pattern, and recalled – all under political control. National command authorities are therefore not confronted with the missile dilemma of 'to launch or not to launch'. Also, bombers are flexible: they can strike at targets of opportunity, conduct strike/reconnaissance missions, and complete the hard-target counter-force task against weapons either pinned down in their silos by the effects of preceding missile strikes or being held in reserve. Moreover, the manned bomber force presents anyone considering a disarming first strike with serious problems over the timing of his attack.[8] The comparatively short flight time of SLBM directed at bomber bases (as low as six minutes) could in theory prevent a large portion of the manned bomber force from attaining its safe escape points, but in practice such a salvo would provide ample warning time for the launch of the *Minuteman* wings. Alternatively, ICBM launched so as to arrive at the same time as SLBM would give generous warning time to the manned bomber force.

It seems very unlikely that SSBN or manned bomber technology will face any imminent obsolescence in the 1980s and 1990s. Therefore, it is assumed in this study that acute problems of pre-launch vulnerability and/or mission completion will not beset the SLBM or manned

---

[7] In keeping with common usage, this study focuses upon those weapon systems which Western governments and analysts describe as *strategic*. However, the United States retains the services of a large inventory of nuclear-capable medium-range bombers and strike aircraft which could, from forward bases (and even without in-flight refuelling), hit targets in the Western Soviet Union. See Uwe Nerlich, *The Alliance and Europe: Part V: Nuclear Weapons and East-West Negotiation*, Adelphi Paper No. 120 (London: IISS, 1976). With suitable refuelling support, the aging Soviet force of Tu-16 *Badger* (755) and the new *Backfire* B (85-plus, half deployed with naval aviation) could also perform creditably as intercontinental bombers. Whether or not *Backfire* could strike at North American targets and return to the Soviet Union *without* refuelling has attracted undue attention, although it is understandable in terms of its relevance to the Strategic Arms Limitation Talks. (The bulk of the American strategic bomber force would refuel in the air *en route* to Soviet targets.) For expansive claims concerning *Backfire's* capability, see Robert L. Pfaltzgraff, Jr. and Jacquelyn K. Davis, *SALT II: Promise or Precipice* (Washington, DC: Center for Advanced International Studies, University of Miami, 1976), p. 20. Assuming a reasonably fuel-economic flight envelope, *Backfire's* range must be presumed to be of the order of 5,000 miles, rather than the 3,500 that has gained currency in open Western sources. The current *Backfire* production rate is believed to be two a month. American forward-based systems (FBS) and Soviet medium bombers comprise perennial 'grey areas' in strategic and arms-control analysis. Soviet leaders probably do not view their medium-range bombers as strategic delivery vehicles, but in large numbers these bombers do provide a considerable safeguard against catastrophic postural error in the region of the strategic triad. This judgment is particularly relevant to the Soviet Union, since the North American Air Defense Command (NORAD) now controls what most defence commentators consider to be little more than a token capability to defend against penetrating bombers (its principal role is to act as a 'coast-guard of the air').

[8] Manned bomber forces, and the B-1 programme in particular, are discussed very critically in Alton M. Quanbeck and Archie L. Wood, *Modernizing the Strategic Bomber Force: Why and How* (Washington DC: Brookings Institution, 1976). This work inspired an informative critique, 'Assessment of Quanbeck-Wood Report' (Washington DC: Air Force Studies and Analysis, Headquarters, USAF, 1976). For a useful exchange of views on the value of the B-1 programme, see articles by John F. McCarthy, Jr. and Archie L. Wood, *International Security*, Vol. 1, No. 2 (Fall 1976), pp. 78–122.

bomber forces (with stand-off weapons) before the end of this century.⁹

The Soviet Union does not maintain a large Long-Range Aviation component in her strategic triad, but – and this only partly depends upon the outcome of the negotiating dispute over *Backfire* B at the Strategic Arms Limitations Talks (SALT) – she could mix her strategic forces to create a greater airborne weapon delivery arsenal. She began to test an SLBM with MIRV – the SS-NX-18 – in 1976; under the likely terms of SALT II and probably beyond, she will be able to mix her strategic forces increasingly seawards if the American hard-target counter-force threat mounts in the mid- and late 1980s.

Each leg of the triad has been modernized in response to actual or, more often, distant and hypothetical threats. However, manned bombers and submarines, unlike silo-housed ICBM, do have very real problems of wear. From the early 1960s at least until the early 1980s, there has been, and will be, no total threat to the pre-launch survivability or prospects for mission completion of any of the legs of the triad. Alarms have been raised, but none have survived close scrutiny, offsetting developments, or simply the passing of time. Many genuine but unexpected vulnerabilities have been discovered and offset.¹⁰ It is quite possible that major vulnerabilities remain to be discovered, a thought which should discipline any great measure of enthusiasm for becoming reliant exclusively, or nearly exclusively, on only one set of technologies – SSBN, for example.

III. DOCTRINE

With the deployment of a generation of high throw-weight MIRV-equipped ICBM (with a circular error probable (CEP) that must be presumed already to be around 0·25 nautical miles or better), the Soviet Union is acquiring the means to eliminate the American fixed-site ICBM force.¹¹ American strategic developments will probably be similar (though at a later date). Figure 1 illustrates the steady improvement in missile accuracy since the early 1960s.

The drive to greater accuracy is fuelled by a number of complementary elements. First, regardless of official doctrine, teams of scientists and engineers do and will inevitably discover ways of improving system performance.¹² For example, without purchasing new hardware (such as precision guidance) or tapping the Global Positioning System (GPS) that is to be deployed in the early 1980s,¹³ the CEP of *Minute-*

---

⁹ Assuming that the B-1 bomber is not bought, this judgment may be false. B-52G/H and wide-bodied jets functioning as stand-off missile launch platforms could suffer severe pre-launch attrition from SLBM fired on depressed trajectories, while the penetration capability of stand-off cruise missiles could be catastrophically low should the Soviet Union deploy mobile low-altitude surface-to-air missiles (which could not be targeted for suppression) and/or an efficient airborne warning and control system (AWACS) controlling a 'look down/shoot down' manned interceptor force.

¹⁰ Electromagnetic pulse (EMP) is a leading example of a long-unrecognized vulnerability. See Fred C. Iklé, 'The Prevention of Nuclear War in a World of Uncertainty', Speech at the Joint Harvard/MIT Arms Control Seminar, 20 February 1974 (ACDA text).

¹¹ Three years ago the US Department of Defense credited the latest generation of Soviet ICBM with CEP in the 0·25–0·3 nm range. US Senate, Committee on Foreign Relations, Subcommittee on Arms Control, International Law and Organization, *Briefing on Counterforce Attacks*, Hearing, 93rd Cong., 2nd sess. (Washington DC: USGPO, 11 September 1974, released 10 January 1975), p. 10. By mid-1977 there was no consensus on the CEP of the SS-17, -18 and -19.

¹² In the words of Jack Ruina: 'On the issue of guidance accuracy, there is no way to get hold of it, it is a laboratory development, and there is no way to stop progress in that field.' US Senate, Committee on Foreign Relations, Subcommittee on International Organization and Disarmament Affairs, *Strategic and Foreign Policy Implications of ABM Systems*, Hearings, Part 3, 91st Cong., 1st sess. (Washington DC: USGPO 1969), p. 672.

¹³ The NAVSTAR GPS is being deployed by stages from 1976–7 until 1984. See 'Range Instrumentation Advances Spurred', *Aviation Week and Space Technology*, Vol. 103, No. 18 (3 November 1975), p. 34; and Barry Miller, 'Defense Navstar Program Progressing', *Aviation Week and Space Technology*, Vol. 104, No. 2 (12 January 1976), pp. 45–7, 49–50. Also of use are Edgar Ulsamer, 'The Pervasive Importance of USAF's Space Mission', *Air Force Magazine*, Vol. 59, No. 1 (January 1976), pp. 48–9; Richard L. Garwin, 'Effective Military Technology for the 1980s', *International Security*, Vol. 1, No. 2 (Fall 1976), pp. 66–71; and Kosta Tsipis, 'Cruise Missiles', *Scientific American*, Vol. 236, No. 2 (February 1977),

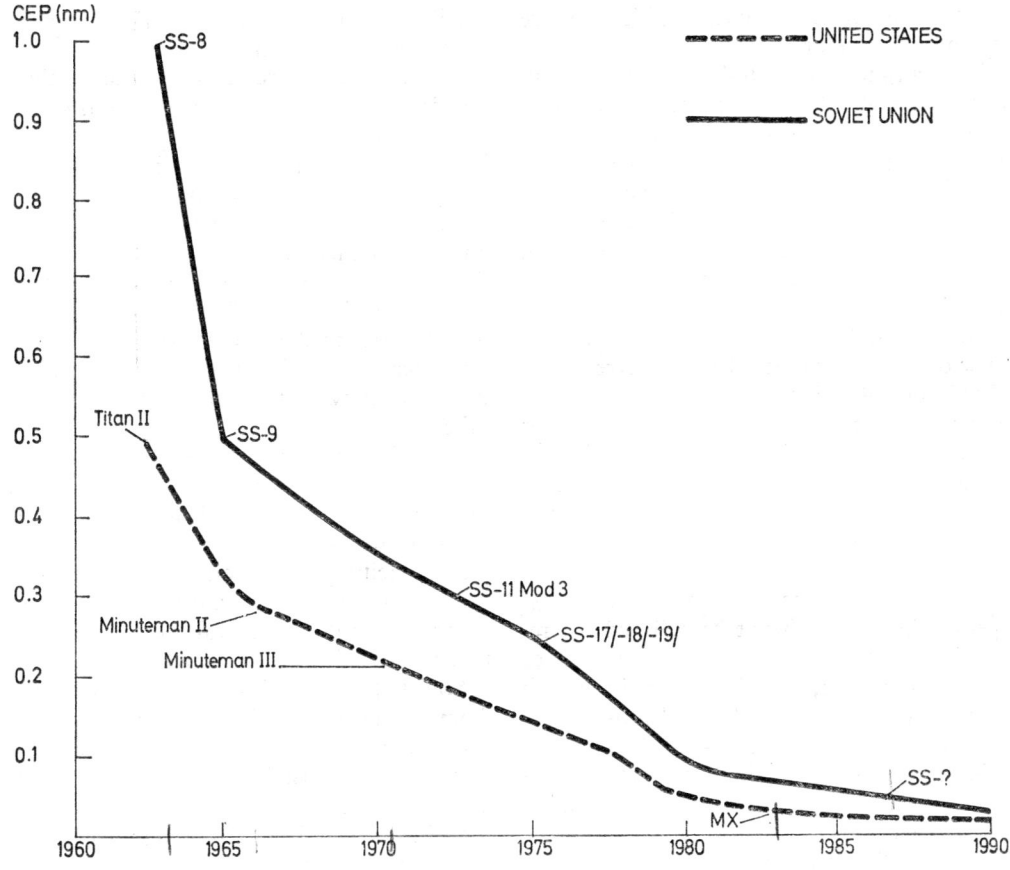

Figure 1: Estimated CEP of ICBM, 1960–90

This Figure represents the judgment of the author, based upon a variety of official, semi-official and unofficial sources. The slopes shown may be incorrect in some details, but the trend to lower CEP is almost certainly indicated with little distortion.

man III will be reduced from around 1,500 ft to approximately 400–600 ft. Second, the United States (and possibly the Soviet Union) has embraced a strategic targeting doctrine which calls for the ability to strike with great precision at a very wide range of targets – with minimum collateral damage.[14] Third, bearing in mind Soviet war-fighting doctrine and the predictable hard-target threat in the MIRV-equipped SS-17/-18/-19 generation of Soviet ICBM, the United States is clearly on record as not being prepared to allow herself to be seriously out-matched in hard-target killing potential, partly for reasons of possible adverse political perceptions.[15] Though there are major differences between Soviet and American strategic doctrine,[16] for divergent reasons the two super-powers are very likely to de-

---

p. 23. The most imformative discussion to date is Douglas Smith and William Criss, 'GPS: Navstar Global Positioning System', *Astronautics and Aeronautics* (April 1976), pp. 26–32.

[14] For example, see Donald H. Rumsfeld, *Annual Defense Department Report, FY 1977* (Washington DC: USGPO, 27 January 1976), pp. 57–9.

[15] 'We have no desire to develop a unilateral counterforce capability against the Soviet Union. [Deleted]. What we wish to avoid is the Soviet Union having a counterforce capability against the United States without our being able to have a comparable capability.' James Schlesinger, *op. cit.* in note 11, p. 3. Whether or not one agrees, this determination has to be viewed as a datum: it has been restated in Rumsfeld, *Annual Defense Department Report, FY 1978* (Washington DC: USGPO, 17 January 1977), pp. 70–2.

[16] See Colin S. Gray, *The Soviet–American Arms Race* (Lexington, Mass.: Lexington Books, 1976), Chapter 3.

velop and maintain strategic capabilities that are not strongly dissimilar.

A deterrent must be credible not merely to an adversary, but also to its political masters, but, beyond its deterrent (and, in Soviet perspective defensive) role, strategic offensive power fulfils diplomatic roles. Two such roles have dominated recent strategic debate – the symbolic and the coercive – though the distinction between them is by no means clear. Deterrence is a product of political judgments; the level and character of threat offered and perceived – which determines whether or not one chooses to be deterred – are deeply political decisions.

In his Defense Report for FY 1976, James Schlesinger wrote of the need to sustain 'an essential equivalence in the basic factors that determine force effectiveness', and 'a range and magnitude of capabilities such that everyone – friend, foe, and domestic audiences alike – will perceive that we are the equal of our strongest competitors'.[17] Exactly what he believed the relationship to be between military competence and diplomatic effect, he did not explain, but he did imply very strongly that all observers – Soviet, American and others – might interpret specific strategic disparities in favour of the Soviet Union, as well as a more substantial-looking Soviet force posture, as evidence of actual or impending decline in the relative influence of the United States. The hypothetical Soviet advantage which he most often emphasized – the ability to strike successfully at hardened military targets – was specified as a potential source of Soviet coercive diplomacy.[18] Should a marked and widely-appreciated asymmetry in hard-target counter-force potential develop, the stronger power might then reap the political benefits (in terms of its foreign policy objectives) of a reputation that rested solely upon promissory actions.

Criticism of the diplomatic utility of 'cosmetic' military 'superiority' has not been lacking. In the judgment of Paul C. Warnke: 'To conclude that we must overcome every Soviet lead despite its lack of military meaning is to accept the rule of illogic. That kind of lead will have political significance only if we act as if it matters.[19] A very similar point has been made by Abram Chayes: 'The efforts of strategic analysis to demonstrate that numerical superiority remains meaningful or that present force levels can be justified in terms of plausible missions – for example, damage limitation or war-fighting capability – have become increasingly laboured and unconvincing. Countries should have little difficulty in drawing the political conclusions. The political value of weapons is ultimately derived from their military significance. If numerical or technical advantage at present levels does not convey the one, it will soon lose the other.'[20]

There is no way of testing the rival propositions on the political meaning of strategic imbalance. One cannot be certain of just how much weight Soviet leaders attach to indices of relative strategic capacity. Nevertheless, Western defence communities should have learned from the SALT experience that Soviet strategic thought must be taken seriously on its own terms.

Soviet strategic thinking is markedly different from strategic thinking in the West. Firstly, Soviet analysts and leaders do not endorse the dominant Western ideas and theories on such central matters as the desirability of parity; the meaning of stability; the requirements for, and meaning of, deterrence; and the dynamics of the arms race.[21] Secondly, Soviet strategic doctrine apparently draws no distinction between the deterrent and the defensive roles of strategic force, while it enthusiastically endorses the idea that relative strategic capabilities have political meaning.[22] Thirdly, it has not evolved noticeably

---

[17] *Annual Defense Department Report, FY 1976 and FY 197T* (Washington DC: USGPO, 5 February 1975), pp. I–13, 14.
[18] *Ibid.*, pp. I-13, 16, II-4, 9–10. This concern is repeated in *op. cit.* in note 14 p. 57.
[19] Paul C. Warnke, 'Apes on a Treadmill', *Foreign Policy*, No. 18 (Spring 1975), p. 15.
[20] Abram Chayes, 'Nuclear Arms Control After the Cold War', *Daedalus*, Vol. 104, No. 3 (Summer 1975), p. 27.
[21] See 'Foremost Soviet Military Journal Emphasizes Continuing Crucial Role of War and Military Might', *Soviet World Outlook*, Vol. 1, No. 2 (13 February 1976), p. 7; and Leon Gouré, Foy D. Kohler and Mose L. Harvey, *The Role of Nuclear Forces in Current Soviet Strategy* (Washington, DC: Center for Advanced International Studies, University of Miami, 1974).
[22] The Soviet Union does not issue a single annual document which provides an authoritative expression of official views, so argument by selective quotation may be hazardous. None the less, see Georgi A. Arbatov, Central Committee member and director of the Institute of the USA and Canada, who has claimed that the Soviet Union is not seeking to surpass the United States in strategic arms (David K. Shipler, 'Soviet Says Buildup in Arms Isn't

over the past decade, despite SALT and the strategic build-up. The Soviet Union has begun to have a plausible capability for giving operational effect to her traditional war-fighting doctrine, so that doctrinal emphasis upon what analysts in the West term a major war-fighting option is fully congruent both with the weapon systems that she has deployed, and with the content of Soviet strategic writings.[23]

The Soviet Union seeks to acquire a strategic posture which should prove useful should war occur, and American perceptions of this imposing posture should maximize deterrent effect. The Soviet continental experience of total war does not encourage enthusiasm for symbolic or bargaining strikes, so the first duty of the military forces would be the attempted 'blunting' of the American ability to damage the Soviet Union. To Western eyes this posture and doctrine look profoundly destabilizing. To Soviet eyes, however, it is responsible and prudent: it reflects neither technological nor conceptual backwardness, nor need it indicate first strike intentions.

The United States, however, is very far indeed from endorsing a war-fighting posture which balances offence and defence. Civil defence programmes continue to be accorded little more than token concern;[24] strategic air defences are so minimal that their neglect gives the Soviet Long-Range Air Force a capability not dissimilar from that enjoyed by Strategic Air Command, despite the numerical and qualitative differentials; and the substantial American lead in ABM technology (five years, at least) that existed in 1972 at the time of SALT I has almost certainly been considerably eroded.[25] A central question for the United States is therefore whether or not it is politically rather than militarily essential to follow the Soviet lead along doctrinal and postural paths that seem to be both expensive and strategically uninteresting. To deploy a hard-target killing force of MX ICBM (for example, 200 in former *Minuteman* III silos and 200–300 in a mobile mode)[26] would certainly not be cheap, as is argued below, and would constitute a direct repudiation of Western stability theory as it has evolved over the past decade.

There are a number of ways of ensuring the survival of a very large retaliatory force, including land-based missiles. By the simple expedient

---

Aimed at Surpassing US', *The New York Times*, 6 February 1977, pp. 1, 6). However, given the political timing of that claim, its obvious connection with the Carter Administration's appraisal of the very tough American national intelligence estimates of 20 December 1976, and Mr Arbatov's general function as *interlocutor*, one would hardly expect him to say anything else. Soviet strategic capabilities speak eloquently for Soviet doctrine, while the primacy of politics runs through most aspects of Soviet defence policy. In contrast, the idea that there should be a political criterion for strategic sufficiency remains unpopular among American commentators on the arms race and SALT. See Edward N. Luttwak, *The Missing Dimension of US Defense Policy: Force, Perceptions and Power*, revised (Washington DC: Defense Advanced Research Projects Agency, ARPA-TIO-76-2, February 1976).

[23] A useful guide to the Soviet literature is William F. Scott, *Soviet Sources of Military Doctrine and Strategy* (New York: Crane, Russak, 1975). For what the Soviet system believes its officer corps should know and believe, see the series of books, 'Soviet Military Thought', translated under the auspices of the United States Air Force. See also Roger W. Barnett, 'Trans-SALT: Soviet Strategic Doctrine', *Orbis*, Vol. XIX, No. 2 (Summer 1975), pp. 533–61; William F. Scott, 'Soviet Military Doctrine and Strategy: Realities and Misunderstandings', *Strategic Review*, Vol. III, No. 3 (Summer 1975), pp. 57–66; and Benjamin S. Lambeth, 'The Sources of Soviet Military Doctrine', in Frank B. Horton III *et al.* (eds), *Comparative Defense Policy* (Baltimore: John Hopkins UP, 1974), pp. 200–16. The standard work, by Soviet evaluation, remains V. D. Sokolovskiy, *Soviet Military Strategy*, 3rd ed., translated and edited by Harriet F. Scott (New York: Crane, Russak, 1975).

[24] An active civil defence programme is a logical corollary of strategic flexibility. See Schlesinger, *op. cit.* in note 17, pp. II-54–7; *op. cit.* in note 11, pp. 54–5; and Rumsfeld, *op. cit.* in note 15, p. 144. The debate on Soviet civil defence which began in the United States in 1976 attracted a familiar cast of contenders. For once it seemed that truth lies in the middle: it seems improbable that Soviet 'war-survival' measures could limit casualties, immediate and longer-term, to 6–8 per cent of the urban population. However, cursory dismissal of those measures as being of no, or very little, political significance seems highly imprudent. Whether or not the Soviet Union is spending over $1 billion a year on civil defence is uncertain (as uncertain as the amount of protection being purchased), but we do know that the United States plans to spend only $90 million on civil defence in FY 1978. Whatever one's doctrinal predilection, there is no doubt that there is a major, and probably growing, asymmetry between the super-powers in their respective abilities to remove many people from immediate nuclear risk.

[25] The state of ballistic missile defence research is assessed in Kenneth J. Stein, 'New Missile Defence Systems Studied', *Aviation Week and Space Technology*, Vol. 105, No. 15 (11 October 1976), pp. 34–6; and Clarence A. Robinson, Jr., 'US Anti-Missile Work Stresses Optics', *Aviation Week and Space Technology*, Vol. 105, No. 10 (6 September 1976), pp. 30–4.

[26] 231 MX ICBM, suitably cross-targeted, could provide 3,003 warheads – allowing two for each of 1,500 Soviet ICBM silos.

of removing most, if not all, American fixed-point, hard military targets, the Soviet Union could be thwarted by a knight's move in the arms race: her SS-17, SS-18 and SS-19 (and their successors) would lack hard targets and would have been extravagantly over-designed for less exacting missions. Moreover, the precise configuration of a strategic posture could be far less important than the perceived willingness to use it. Limited strategic options (LSO) are not technically incompatible with a force smaller and less sophisticated than that which the United States seems very likely to endorse, but the American exercise of LSO could provoke a Soviet strategic reply that would leave an American President without strategic choices that held promise of promoting an early end to war on an acceptable basis.[27] Although Soviet strategic doctrine may fairly be labelled 'war-fighting' in orientation, as opposed to deterrent (in Western terms), heavy emphasis should not be placed upon the hypothetical dynamics of a limited strategic war. It is more plausible to think of the Soviet posture in terms of counter-deterrence for the discouragement of unwanted escalation. Soviet strategic forces may be intended to hold the ring for the relatively free employment of political and economic pressure, and even the exercise of conventional and theatre nuclear forces in Europe, the Middle East and North-East Asia. Western perceptions of the imposing strategic nuclear options open to the Soviet Union should, therefore, encourage Western governments to define 'local' conflict very much in local terms. This is not to suggest that Soviet political leaders distinguish between usable (conventional and perhaps theatre nuclear) force and unusable (strategic nuclear) force, only that the greater the perceived relative strategic weight of the Soviet Union, the less likely will Western powers be to consider their strategic forces usable – even in very limited and flexible ways.

In my opinion the United States cannot prudently acquiesce in the Soviet development of a superior hard-target counter-force capability. If the United States purchases a matching competence (deployed survivably, i.e. in a land-mobile mode) she will remove the 'peacetime' political deficit that otherwise might ensue, and this should enable a President to use limited strategic options in support of NATO allies in Europe, secure in the knowledge that he could not easily be trumped by a Soviet counter-force reply. It is my belief that the causes of international security, world peace and, if necessary, early war termination favourable to the West, will be well served by an American strategic force posture which creates useful anxiety in Soviet minds. Specifically, a force of survivable land-based ICBM, dedicated to the hard-target mission, would deprive the Soviet Union of a totally effective strategic counter-deterrent and of a devastating (and prospectively war-winning) countermove to American limited strategic options in aid of European allies and would provide Soviet political leaders with the most persuasive of reasons for negotiating seriously in the Strategic Arms Limitation Talks.

IV. STRATEGIC POSTURE: THE RANGE OF CHOICE

The super-powers confront a common dilemma: what is to be done about the growing vulnerability of silo-housed missiles? The possible solutions do not present themselves as a set of discrete alternatives that may be analysed solely on strategic grounds. Considerations of military prudence, bureaucratic and domestic politics, political assessments of strategic appearances, and doctrinal flexibility point rather to a mix of alternative force structures. In simplified form the range of choice is:

1. To phase out silo-housed ICBM without replacement and move to a strategic dyad of SSBN and bombers.
2. To keep them but supplement them from a variety of policies:
   (a) modernize *Minuteman*; (b) change nothing; (c) adopt new firing tactics (launch-on-warning or launch-through-attack); (d) defend silos with ABM; (e) superharden silos; (f) replace present missiles with larger numbers of smaller-payload mini-ICBM.

---

[27] See Benjamin S. Lambeth, *Selective Nuclear Options in American and Soviet Strategic Policy* (Santa Monica, Cal.: Rand Corporation, R-2034-DDRE, December 1976).

3. To phase out silo-housed ICBM and replace them with land- or air-mobile ICBM or air- and/or sea-launched cruise missiles.

In terms of strategic technological (as opposed to political) forecasting, ten to fifteen years is no very great time span. Despite the uncertainties that still pertain to SALT II and to a possible SALT III, the structure and even much of the character of super-power strategic postures in the late 1980s can be predicted with considerable confidence. Until then SSBN and manned bombers (some equipped with stand-off weapons, ballistic and air-breathing) should be able to penetrate to their targets. Air defences and anti-submarine warfare (ASW) will both improve, but such improvement should be neutralized effectively by the very small radar cross-sections of the short-range attack missiles (SRAM) and the air-launched cruise missile (ALCM),[28] and by the greater range of the *Trident* I and II SLBM and the many improvements incorporated in *Trident*-class SSBN. In short, there is no plausible threat on the horizon to two legs of the triad.[29]

Move to a Dyad

As a unilateral measure, or under the auspices of a bilateral regime of arms reduction, either super-power could therefore elect to move to a strategic dyad of SSBN and manned bombers. With predictable improvements in submarine navigation systems, SLBM fitted with precision-guided re-entry vehicles (PGRV) should be able to achieve CEP almost as low as those that would be attainable by the MX ICBM.[30] Without PGRV, it is improbable that SLBM could become satisfactory hard-target killers in the 1980s;[31] even with the benefit of stellar navigation, *Trident* II is unlikely to be able to achieve a single-shot kill probability of much better than 0·75 against targets hardened to withstand 900 pounds per square inch (psi) overpressure. In addition, SSBN have (and almost certainly will continue to have) serious problems of communication, and *Trident* II, if purchased at all, will not be available in large numbers much before 1989–90.

The super-power which first phased out its land-based ICBM would therefore lack a major and fully reliable *rapid* hard-target counter-force capability. However, it could be argued that such a capability would then not be needed: the other super-power would be acutely short of hard targets to threaten. The super-power with a dyad would certainly have conceded a unilateral capability to its adversary, but, with the phasing out of silos, that capability could not be exercised.

A decision not to replace silo-housed ICBM could, however, have important negative consequences. Above all, the damage-limiting task of the adversary would be eased dramatically – assuming that the discarded ICBM were not replaced by other weapons. The adversary would have two, not three, categories of problems upon which to expend his research and development resources, and attack timing would be vastly simplified if the alert bomber force were no longer protected by the time needed for hard-target killers to complete their trajectories from the Soviety Union to the ICBM fields. In addition, the side which retained its ICBM force would enjoy escalation dominance. Soviet leaders might come to believe that a counter-force first strike on a United States with a dyad would stand a reasonable chance of achieving a clear political victory. (It is not implied that the Soviet Union would seriously aspire to effect a total counter-force strike – only that Soviet bargaining strength for intra-war deterrence should be very great indeed after a surprise attack on an American dyad of SSBN and manned bombers.) Soviet leaders would, of course, need to calculate that the United States would co-operate and choose to be deterred in such a situation; however, they

---

[28] Defenders of the B-1 and ALCM programmes have placed very considerable emphasis upon the small radar cross-sections of those systems, but of far greater importance is the penetration survivability of SRAM – which is the principal active-defence suppression weapon for the manned bomber force and ALCM.

[29] This is a qualified judgment. If the United States Air Force were allowed to deploy the B-1 and to fit ALCM to late-model B-52 bombers, then the judgment needs no qualification. However, as the United States has abandoned the B-1 programme and will rely instead on modernized B-52 bombers and wide-bodied jets adapted as ALCM carriers, one should be far less confident that 'the bomber will always get through'.

[30] On *Trident* navigation, see 'Study Finds Joint MX/Trident Impractical', *Aviation Week and Space Technology*, Vol. 103, No. 15 (13 October 1975), p. 17; and 'Trident Subsystem Tests in Final Phase', *Ibid.*, No. 18 (3 November 1975), p. 38.

[31] However, the counter-force potential of SSBN is increasing markedly. See Desmond J. Ball, 'The Counterforce Potential of American SLBM Systems', *Journal of Peace Research*, Vol. XIV, No. I (1977), pp. 23–40.

could aim to achieve a nuclear Pearl Harbour against the 40 per cent or more of the *Poseidon–Trident* fleet that is always in its home ports or at forward bases (Holy Loch and Guam) and hope to catch a large fraction of the B-52/FB-111A force before it could reach its safe escape points, thus leaving the United States Government in a terrible dilemma.

In the face of a major Soviet attempt to interdict shore, air and satellite–SSBN communications, it would be very difficult indeed to wield the SLBM force with any great measure of precision. Moreover, since the Soviet Union would have had knowledge of the American decision to phase out her land-based ICBM force a number of years in advance, a major effort would certainly have been made in the ASW field. With a large force of hunter-killer submarines pre-positioned for attrition of the SSBN force,[32] time would not be on the side of the United States. The Soviet Union might be able to win (old-fashioned though that may sound) a slow-motion counter-force war. The bombers (and tankers) and SSBN that survived the opening blow and which could be reached by (and acknowledge) instructions would be pitted against a society that, presumably, had evacuated its major cities and had its air defences in maximum readiness. In such a desperate situation, what targets would an American President dare to strike? If this were to occur in the mid- rather than the late 1980s (that is, before *Trident* II had been fully deployed), then an American hard-target killing response would be an exercise in progressive unilateral disarmament.[33]

There are flaws in the above scenario. The attack-warning problem for the Soviet Union of striking simultaneously at geographically very dispersed SSBN home ports and bases and at bomber bases has been ignored. Also, there should be no way in which a sneak SLBM attack, even on depressed trajectories, could evade detection by the Defense Satellite Program (DSP) and by the new *Pave Paw* phased-array SLBM warning radars on the North American littoral. Furthermore,

although communication with SSBN at sea is less than perfect, an adversary could not be certain that he could sever or degrade that communication adequately. Finally, although intra-war deterrence should function to the Soviet advantage, with the United States unable to execute either large-scale hard-target killing options or small and very small LSO, except with manned bombers, it would be in keeping with the Soviet philosophy of war for Soviet leaders to expect the United States to do as much damage as she could. The above scenario, although imperfect, does illustrate how the waging of a central nuclear war could become a great deal more 'thinkable' if a well-appointed triad was opposed to a dyad. A strategic posture must be designed to deter in the worst plausible case, not in the best.

Quite apart from the critical communications weaknesses which SSBN have unless they approach the surface, and thus risk detection, it is unlikely that a United States resorting to a dyad would look the equal of a Soviet Union that maintained her triad. Although the United States might retain the ability to assure the destruction of Soviet society and the Soviet state (provided Soviet civil defence programmes are much less efficient in practice than they are on paper), the Soviet Union would still enjoy the uncertain benefits of a more capable strategic posture. Moreover, as the United States came to rely upon her SSBN and manned bombers, there would be a prolonged period before the major deployment of *Trident* II during which the major part of the Soviet ICBM force, in its silos, would not be vulnerable to American hard-target counter-force action.

Although the arguments for a strategic dyad of SSBN and manned bombers are strong, the strategic and political reasons for retaining a triad (at least) are rather more weighty. Strategically, a dyad must increase the opponent's chances of success for a variety of first strike counter-force options. Such options need not include a bid for total disarming success: partial enforced disarmament, paralysis of the strategic chain of command and intra-war deterrence or coercion could well be 'good enough'. It is true that SLBM with PGRV could accomplish surgical strikes for political bargaining ends, but no government could be assured of its ability to convey precise, detailed and timely targeting instructions to the

---

[32] However, this prepositioning, would entail such a significant deviation from normal Soviet deployment practice that appropriate counter measures should not be difficult to effect.

[33] That is to say, the greater the weight of the American attack, the more advantageous for the Soviet Union would be the balance of residual throw-weight.

few SSBN that would be suitably located.³⁴ Bombers or cruise missiles could carry out LSO, but they would be relatively slow to their targets and very actively opposed (particularly in the absence of large-scale defence suppression strikes). Politically, it would be difficult to convince public opinion that (as an expression of political will as much as strategic capabilities) a dyad was the equal of a triad.

From time to time it is suggested that dyad versus triad arguments rest upon the false premise that there is a simple choice. One could place second-strike reliance upon SLBM and manned bombers, constituting a dyad for major retaliatory purposes, while retaining a theoretically vulnerable silo-housed ICBM force for some LSO tasks, general weight in peacetime perceptions, and synergistic value for launch-on-warning (LOW) bomber resources. Hence, the strategic forces could be thought of as having a two-and-a-half part structure. This is not a ridiculous suggestion, but the vulnerability of ICBM would virtually guarantee a very large counter-strike indeed against the ICBM fields in the American homeland if any American strategic forces executed LSO. The enemy would be offered a military option on a major scale that he should be able to effect successfully.

Leave Silo-housed ICBM in Place

Modernize Minuteman

If the United States decides to leave fixed-site ICBM in place indefinitely, a choice must be made as to whether or not the 1,000 *Minuteman* II and III and 54 *Titan* II are to be replaced, in whole or in part, by an MX follow-on system. The *Minuteman* III production line is still open, and this missile could be fitted with AIRS³⁵ or PGRV,³⁶ should very low CEP be desired. The much higher throw-weight of the MX would offer a more substantial and assured hard-target kill potential, with a CEP approaching 100–300 ft and a wide range of possible payload subdivisions, but, since few people are interested in waging an ICBM counter-force duel of attrition, it might be judged that *Minuteman* III would be quite sufficient. The throw-weight differential would grow greatly to the American disadvantage, as the SS-17, -18 and -19 series was deployed in very large numbers, but the limited utility of throw-weight comparisons as an index of strategic potency is widely realized.³⁷

This is not to say that throw-weight is unimportant, only that *Minuteman* III could be judged to have a gowth potential in the hard-target counter-force area that would be fully adequate for American purposes.³⁸ Backfitted with AIRS and with the force expanded to 1,000 (replacing the 450 *Minuteman* II), *Minuteman* III could target the entire Soviet ICBM deployment, with 3,000 warheads divided among approximately 1,500 aiming points.³⁹ Even with

---

to improve CEP, not simply to evade possible ABM. Despite the change in official labels, PGRV refers in this paper to terminally-guided re-entry vehicles. See Barry Miller, 'Advanced Re-entry Vehicle Tests Planned', *Aviation Week and Space Technology*, Vol. 104, No. 21 (24 May 1976), pp. 22–3.

³⁷ The standard, simplified counter-force formula of $K = Y^{2/3}/(CEP)^2$ means, as a rough and ready rule, that an improvement in accuracy (CEP) by half is the equivalent in terms of counter-force effectiveness of an eight-fold increase in yield. Reacting to what it deemed undue public devaluation in the importance attached to throw-weight, the Department of Defense has issued what it clearly hoped was an effective brief rejoinder. See US Senate, Committee on Foreign Relations, Subcommittee on US Security Agreements and Commitments Abroad, *Nuclear Weapons and Foreign Policy*, 93rd Cong., 2nd Sess. (Washington DC: USGPO, 1974), p. 170. The terse document in question bears the innocuous, if rather indigestible, title, 'Principles Affecting Throw-weight vs Accuracy Trade-off Calculations'. However, given that Henry Kissinger expressed the opinion that 'throw-weight is a phony issue' ('Background Briefing on SALT', 3 December 1974, mimeo., p. A-2), the 'Principles' paper must be seen as a political statement.

³⁸ This view is defended in detail in Donald R. Westervelt, 'The Essence of Armed Futility', *Orbis*, Vol. XVIII, No. 3 (Fall 1974), pp. 689–705.

³⁹ This is the figure for the end of FY 1977 for Soviet ICBM deployment. Under the terms of the Interim Agreement of SALT I, there is a 'conversion ceiling' of 1,339 for ICBM – meaning that (heavy) ICBM deployed prior to 1964 may be 'exchanged' for SLBM. The Soviet Union had 209

---

³⁴ The LSO that Schlesinger advertised so robustly tended to be very small strikes, well below the scale embraced in the single integrated operational plan (SIOP). With that in mind, it is worth noting that SLBM bearing 7, 8, 10 or 14 warheads could be inadequately fitted to fire symbolic shots at very small target systems.

³⁵ See glossary, also Barry Miller, 'MX Guidance Elements in Development', *Aviation Week and Space Technology*, Vol. 105, No. 24 (13 December 1976), pp. 67–70, 75–6.

³⁶ See glossary. At least five different kinds of sensors are currently (1977) under study for the PGRV mission in the Advanced Ballistic Re-entry Systems (ABRES) programme. PGRV has been re-named AMARV (for Advanced Manoeuvrable Re-entry Vehicle), but the former initials were more informative because the programme is attempting

silos hardened to 1,500 psi, only a handful of Soviet ICBM should survive.

The case for an MX follow-on to the *Minuteman* series rests overwhelmingly upon the greater flexibility of targeting accorded by a throw-weight that would be at least four times as great as for the current *Minuteman* III. If 'counter-force matching' was the principal task, then the United States would either have to proliferate *Minuteman* III or else fractionate payload very considerably for any additional missions to be planned. With a force level of 1,000 *Minuteman* III, appropriately upgraded, the United States could barely match Soviet hard-target kill competence: there would be no ICBM warheads to spare for economic, political or military targets other than silos. If the yield of (some) *Minuteman* warheads were to be reduced to, for example, 40 kilotons (KT), the weight penalties (and possible vulnerability to jamming) of precision guidance and manoeuvring technologies would have to be accepted. For truly precise guidance, in the foreseeable future, some form of radiation sensing will have to be employed – and any radiation sensing system may be jammed. Also, the more manoeuvrable a re-entry vehicle, the slower it will go, and hence the more vulnerable it will be to active defences.

The case for modernizing land-based missile forces is not difficult to appreciate: at the most basic level, by the late 1980s the average age of the *Minuteman* III force will be fifteen years. None the less, the upgrading of the *Minuteman* force on a scale more extensive than is planned at present does remain a possible policy option.

When the debate over the mobile MX is fully joined over the next few years, the arguments mentioned above are almost certain to be raised. *Minuteman* III will be found to have major growth potential as a hard-target killer.[40] The low throw-weight of *Minuteman* III (2,000 lb) relative to that of MX (8–10,000 lb) will probably be held to be irrelevant, given the expected dramatic improvements in CEP. Many of the claims likely to be made on behalf of an upgraded *Minuteman* III will have some plausibility, but they should be assessed in the light of the following considerations: the fifteen-year-old system might have or develop some major and possibly unrecognized reliability problems; one could not have great confidence in the ability of all-inertial guidance systems to deliver CEPs in the required range of 0·05–0·1 nm; and it may be difficult to render terminal guidance secure against countermeasures. An MX with a warhead of far higher yield than the Mk 12A (340KT) would provide a hard-target kill potential in which great confidence could be placed. The higher yield of MX warheads could compensate for the residual uncertainties over the performance of all-inertial guidance, while the higher throw-weight would greatly ease the task of accommodating precision-guidance technology. Furthermore, investment in an MX programme would be seen by the Soviet defence community, and others, as a clear signal that the United States declined to acquiesce in a growing Soviet hard-target kill capability. However fundamentally it was upgraded, *Minuteman* III (or IV) improvement would lack the political impact of MX – a new programme. Finally, the promise in an upgraded *Minuteman* III programme is threatened by probable SALT constraints. The Vladivostok ceilings provide only for 1,320 MIRV launchers.[41] It is implausible to suggest that the United States would use 1,000 of her allowance in a land-based mode (particularly on a system such as *Minuteman* III, whose target coverage was so seriously restricted by comparatively low throw-weight).

Change Nothing

All analysts are aware of the possibility (of unknown, and even unknowable dimensions) that 'things will go wrong on the night'. 'Change nothing' should not be interpreted as a stance of

---

ICBM that qualified for this conversion (the SS-7/-8). The American baseline figure for Soviet ICBM strength under SALT I is 1,608. When and if SALT II comes to pass, both parties might be able to convert their ICBM forces into SLBM to whatever degree they choose. In 1977, it is impossible to predict the level of Soviet ICBM deployment for the mid-1980s. However, indications that it will be very substantial include the known facts of a major silo upgrading programme (to psi resistance values of at least 2,000), and an annual deployment rate for SS-17/-18/-19 of more than 100 a year.

[40] The scope for improvement may be demonstrated thus: against an upgraded, modified SS-17, SS-18 or SS-19 silo hardened to withstand (at least) 2,000 psi, the single-shot kill probability of a Mk 12 (170KT) re-entry vehicle of a *Minuteman* III with a CEP estimated to be close to 0·15 nm would be only 25 per cent. If two Mk 12 warheads are employed, the ceiling for high-confidence avoidance of fratricide problems, the kill probability rises to nearly 44 per cent.

[41] While SALT II is expected to specify a MIRV-launcher sub-limit 820 for ICBM.

rigid conservatism: rather as one of benign neglect. Modest improvements in the ability of ICBM launchers to withstand nuclear-weapon effects would be carried out, but no major programmes of silo super-hardening or active defence would be undertaken; missiles in place would be phased out only to be replaced by follow-on fixed-site systems; and no radical departures in firing tactics would be adopted. The reasons for this relatively inactive response to a growing threat include the following: no one can be confident that he comprehends fully the many elements of the fratricide problem,[42] let alone that he had designed very reliable solutions to them; a small-scale hard-target attack would succeed, but such an attack could easily be answered in kind; even if the fratricide problem were to be solved finally, the sources of cumulative error that create ineffectiveness are many and should be expected to evade prior compensating actions (for example, via cross-targeting);[43] and, given the relative invulnerability of manned bombers and SSBN, it is not credible that either side would launch a major disarming strike at ICBM silos. The consideration of strategic appearances would favour this option. The United States would retain the cheapest means for effecting first strike counter-force and would maintain a strategic posture which looked sufficiently symmetrical to that of the adversary. Moreover, in terms of the attack-timing problem an ICBM force, regardless of its basing mode, ensures that manned bombers will receive adequate warning.

If states were always governed by level-headed and reasonable men who were strongly disinclined (under all foreseeable circumstances) to take grave risks, the above arguments would be strong. However, leaders are not always level-headed and reasonable, and the option of benign inattention could prove to be fatal. Experts differ, but there are many to be found in the West (and presumably in the East) who do not believe that the problems of fratricide or operational CEP degradation are beyond solution. With one (and possibly both) sides believing that it could destroy the ICBM leg of the adversary's triad, one could be dangerously close to the Pearl Harbour analogy. As Paul Wolfowitz has argued, one may find

> the irrational concentration on a neatly 'rational' solution to what may in fact be only a part of the total problem facing the decision-maker.... Thus, within a crisis situation produced by other more fundamental causes, the development of a brilliant plan offering a chance of crippling the US Pacific fleet became a major factor in tipping the Japanese decision toward war. This is part of the reason for present-day concern about allowing the land-based components of the US deterrent force to become temptingly vulnerable, even though a substantial and still relatively secure deterrent would survive on board nuclear submarines at sea. The fear is that in a desperate situation an adversary might be tempted by the prospect of a successful initial attack against the land-based forces – trusting to luck, or to communication delays, or to 'nuclear blackmail' to solve the problems of the submarines.[44]

This may seem to be far-fetched, as indeed it is, but probably most strategic analysts would deem it unwise to offer for an adversary's first-strike attention such a substantial target system as the entire ICBM leg of the triad. The perception that ICBM were (in theory, at least) vulnerable to a first strike should more than offset any political benefit secured by not evacuating silos under the threat of vulnerability.

It has to be presumed, on the evidence of deployment and known research and development activity, that the Soviet Union is bent upon achieving a total hard-target kill capability (for whatever reasons). The 'best' current American intelligence estimate predicts that theoretical accomplishment for 1984-85. The 'change nothing' option means that should the Soviet Union seek and achieve that capability, she would acquire an enormous first-strike bonus. The Soviet Union could still be severely damaged by the remainder of the triad, a prospect which may provide all

---

[42] See glossary for an explanation of the fratricide problem.

[43] See glossary. Counter-force graphs devised by the Department of Defense in 1974 made explicit allowance for operational CEP degradation *as high as* 0·1 and 0·2 nm. Senate Committee on Foreign Relations, Sub-committee on Arms Control, International Law and Organization, *US–USSR Strategic Policies, Hearing*, 93rd Cong., 2nd Sess. (Washington DC: USGPO, 4 April 1974), p. 16. There will always be a range of expected CEP, depending upon the trajectories selected. Within the US defence community there are analysts closely concerned with the problem who are very sceptical about the very low CEP values that have become familiar in recent years.

[44] 'The Pot and the Kettle, or Rationality Within Reason: Mr Green's Deadly Logic', in Morton A. Kaplan (ed.), *Strategic Thinking and Its Moral Implications* (Chicago: Center for Policy Study, University of Chicago Press, 1973), p. 78.

the deterrent effect that the United States needs. However, I believe – and these assessments cannot be fully verified – that a hard-target counter-force imbalance of major proportions might be deemed by Soviet leaders to license a more adventurous style and content in their diplomacy.[45]

Adopt Launch-on-Warning or Launch-through-attack Firing Tactics

LOW/LTA firing tactics offer a deceptively simple and economical solution to the problem of silo vulnerability. Parked in synchronous equatorial orbits over the Eastern and Western hemispheres, satellites of the 949-647 Defense Satellite Program (DSP) would transmit near real-time notice of a missile attack, and their information should be in the hands of the President within three to four minutes of satellite detection (the first step towards deployment of a parallel Soviet system was reportedly taken on 8 October 1975 with the launching of *Cosmos* 775 into geo-stationary orbit).[46] If American missiles were immediately launched, the adversary would face the prospect of striking at empty silos – which perhaps offers the maximum possible discouragement to nuclear adventure.

Arguments for LOW were totally demolished in the course of the protracted ABM debate, particularly by Paul Wolfowitz,[47] but, properly handled, LOW has some deterrent merit. As an operational firing tactic, it would be a monumental folly, but as a veiled suggestion of the 'we refuse to rule it out' variety it should not be despised. Responsible decision-makers must retain a small suspicion that the adversary might just launch some missiles before the incoming warheads arrived: one should not attempt totally to allay this suspicion. Also, LOW could prove to be a valuable backstop if either super-power found itself temporarily embarrassed by technical surprise or tardy arms race response.

As anything more than a short-term expedient, however, LOW contains very undesirable features. It would require an instant retaliatory response, leaving no time for the selection of appropriate targets, and would require the President or the Politburo to act on warning signals which might not be totally reliable. Early-warning satellites (which contain infra-red sensors, visible light detectors and particle and radiation sensors) might be blinded or attacked:[48] would such action be judged to be the equivalent of early warning or a missile attack? Simultaneously, one or more of the three Ballistic Missile Early-Warning System facilities could be destroyed – thus leaving the United States with no reliable early-warning capabilities *vis-à-vis* the principal missile threat 'windows'. If a super-power did not launch its ICBM in response to the destruction of key early-warning facilities, the tactic of LOW could not thereafter be implemented. Even more worrying than the distant possibility of attempts to degrade early-warning systems would be the prospect of war by accident. Early-warning satellites, for all their many virtues, are prone to registering solar reflection as the plumes from rocket engines.

Launch-through-attack is a more sophisticated relation of LOW. It presumes that an adversary would not so time his missile launches that they all impacted simultaneously over and on missile fields and bomber bases. Human and technical error and a very deliberate attempt to preclude widespread fratricidal effects should ensure that warhead arrivals would be sequential to some

---

[45] Donald Rumsfeld has written: 'Before our deterrent can be credible to him [an adversary], it must be credible to us' (*op. cit.* in note 14, p. 56). This need not be true, but Soviet analysts reading official American strategic prose can hardly fail to note the extreme scepticism expressed over the relevance of a counter-city response to a counter-force strike (see *ibid.*, p. 57). If the United States were to decide to retain her ICBM in their silos, the denigration of counter-city responses should be halted promptly.

[46] *Aviation Week and Space Technology*, Vol. 103, No. 20 (17 November 1975), p. 13; and US Senate, Committee on Aeronautical and Space Sciences, *Soviet Space Programs, 1971–75*, Staff Report by the Science Policy Research Division, Congressional Research Service, Library of Congress, 94th Cong., 2nd sess. (Washington DC: USGPO, 30 August 1976), p. 607, also see the discussion on pp. 388–9.

[47] 'The proposal to Launch on Warning', in US Senate, Committee on Armed Services, *Authorization for Military Procurement, Research and Development, Fiscal Year 1971, and Reserve Strength, Hearings*, Part 3, 91st Cong., 2nd sess. (Washington DC: USGPO, 1970), pp. 2278–82.

[48] The United States Air Force is now approaching the end of a four-year programme devoted to the development of anti-satellite technology. Among the concepts being explored are infra-red homing satellite interceptors and large metallic nets. See 'USAF Studies Spacecraft Survivability', *Aviation Week and Space Technology*, Vol. 103, No. 5 (4 August 1975), pp. 41–2, for details of defensive developments; and Barry J. Smernoff, *Channeling High Energy Laser Technology Through Arms Control: Some Critical Ambiguities* (Croton, NY: Hudson Institute, HI-2549-P, 8 December 1976).

degree. Rather than launching on warning alone, a super-power could afford to sit out the entire flight time of the first salvos, permit some warheads to complete their missions, and then – on the basis of some minimal exercise in attack assessment – launch through the follow-on salvos. LTA would preclude the possibility of launching on the basis of erroneous information and should give possibly as long as half an hour in which to consider an appropriate response. By the 1980s it might prove feasible to upgrade the capability of the DSP so that launches from particular silos could be identified (though a launch would have to be discovered within a very few seconds for this to be possible).

LTA calls for strong nerves and a certain technical optimism. Whereas LOW cannot be thwarted by adversary action (assuming that destruction of vital early-warning facilities would be treated as a *casus belli*), LTA positively invites offsetting ingenuity. Faced with an LTA firing tactic, an aspiring first striker could design his first missile salvos for maximum 'pin-down' effect (the weapon effects which produce fratricide would also preclude ICBM launches) pending the arrival of the serious hard-target killing force. While it would be difficult to design such an attack, one would be some way from the deterring certainty of retaliation inherent in a rigorously applied LOW tactic.

Defend with Anti-Ballistic Missiles

In the ABM Treaty of SALT I the Soviet Union provided convincing evidence of the respect she accorded American ABM technology. Since May 1972 she has undertaken research and development on all aspects of ABM problems – activities which led inevitably to charges in the United States that she has violated either the terms of the ABM Treaty, or its spirit as communicated by Henry Kissinger and others to the Congress.[49]

Whether or not the Soviet Union was guilty as charged (and the evidence is highly ambiguous), the scale and vigour of her ABM endeavours are not matched in the United States.[50] In addition to research and development into strategic ABM systems, she is also energetically pursuing R&D of tactical or theatre-oriented ABM technology.

Now that the heat and fury which characterized the ABM debate in the late 1960s have passed, the strategic value of advanced ABM technologies should be seriously reconsidered. The blanket claim that ABM defences of any character are destabilizing is unlikely to gain many adherents in the late 1970s. The ABM technology of the mid- to late 1980s would not be the technology that was debated in 1969. For example, a superpower deploying defences for some hard targets (so that the silos to be defended could not be identified in advance by an attacker) could field an ABM system of quick-reaction interceptor missiles fitted with multiple non-nuclear warheads that would home on to their targets. Developments of the *Site Defense* radar currently being installed for prototype demonstration at Kwajalein Atoll would provide systems capable of discriminating between ICBM tank fragments, heavy decoys (the principal discrimination problem) and the particular warheads carried by the SS-16–19 series of ICBM.

It is likely that the Soviet Union would take an advanced American ABM system very seriously indeed. She would undoubtedly be hostile, initially, to an American proposal that the ABM Treaty be fundamentally revised, but, as Soviet leaders come to appreciate more fully the hard-target killing implications of AIRS and PGRV technologies, they could well decide that countervailing hard-point defences would be strategically preferable to (and a great deal less costly than) a race for new mobile ICBM basing modes. Such defences might aggravate the war-fighting problems of the Soviet Union considerably, but a proliferation of American land- or air-mobile ICBM (with the addition of cruise missiles) would do the same.

---

[49] The SALT 'violations' debate, fed largely by means of 'leaks' to *Aviation Week and Space Technology*, rumbled on in public from the Autumn of 1974 until early 1976. Useful testimony was offered by Schlesinger in US Senate, Committee on Armed Services, Subcommittee on Arms Control, *Soviet Compliance with Certain Provisions of the 1972 SALT I Agreements, Hearing*, 94th Cong., 1st sess. (Washington DC: USGPO, 6 March 1975). See also Walter Slocombe, 'Learning from Experience: Verification Guidelines for SALT II', *Arms Control Today*, Vol. 6, No. 2 (February 1976), pp. 1–6; Jan M. Lodal, 'Verifying SALT', *Foreign Policy*, No. 24 (Fall 1976), pp. 40–64; and *Strategic Survey 1975* (London: IISS, 1976), pp. 114–16.

[50] See Clarence A. Robinson: 'Soviets Push ABM Development', *Aviation Week and Space Technology*, Vol. 102, No. 14 (7 April 1975), pp. 12–14; and his article 'Soviets Grasping Strategic Lead', *Aviation Week and Space Technology*, Vol. 105, No. 9 (30 August 1976), pp. 14–18.

Within the next few decades, a large-scale network of laser-armed satellites might be the most effective ABM system. However, development of a laser ABM weapon system is well beyond the present state of the art, and (perhaps more telling) such a system would run the risk of being 'too good', in that it would threaten all ballistic missiles, whatever their intended targets, as well as all aircraft flying above cloud level. However, when satellite-housed laser ABM weapons do become practicable, the race to develop and deploy satellite killers will assume a frenetic pace.[51]

The existence of the 1972 ABM Treaty leads many people to dismiss the possibilities of ABM defending ICBM silos. But since the strategic purpose of SALT, at least on the American side, is the technical stabilization of the strategic balance, it would be unwise to eschew any promising site-defence options solely because of probable incompatibility with the treaty;[52] the political ramifications of seeking amendments to the ABM Treaty might be adverse, but a strategic situation marked by sharply growing, and eventually reciprocal, hard-target counter-force capabilities seems likely to do very little for the health of Soviet–American relations either. Site-defence technology does not necessarily have to be sophisticated and hence very expensive. Richard Garwin, for example, has suggested the development of a 'pebble-fan projector' which would destroy or disable incoming re-entry vehicles (RV). On radar detection, the RV would be assaulted by a ten-ton barrage of steel pellets, 'providing a projected density of 10 pellets per square metre over a protective screen 300 metres square, providing a high probability of dudding or detonating a hypersonic RV'.[53] Technical opinions vary as to how easily Garwin's pebble-fan could be countered.

A major reason why ABM site-defence options look less promising in 1977 than they did in 1969 is that the SALT process has failed either to constrain missile payload to any important degree or to control significantly the scale upon which that payload may be sub-divided. The only assured penetration tactic against an ABM defence is to exhaust all the available interceptor missiles. At present, it seems likely that the Soviet ICBM force alone will be able to dispense close to 8,000 high-yield warheads in the 1980s. If Soviet planners foresaw their threat to *Minuteman* silos being significantly hindered by ABM, a drastic fractionation of the payload of their modern ICBM could be achieved.

Terminal ABM defence of silos does not, therefore, look promising for the 1980s: the scale and sophistication of the threat has probably outrun 'the state of the art' in the active defence field. None the less, 'unconventional' terminal defence ideas should be encouraged – just as so-called 'exotic' anti-missile concepts (e.g. high-energy laser and particle-beam technologies) should be monitored closely. This generally sceptical appraisal of ABM prospects, however, relates solely to the site defence type of system deployed in defence of silos. A very different judgment might be reached about preferential point defences for complexes of land-mobile ICBM – particularly in the context of a hypothetical SALT regime which set severe limits upon missile throw-weight. A well-designed land-mobile deployment should require an adversary to resort to a saturation attack (on all 'occupiable' ICBM shelters) which would either overstrain, or strain to the limit, his ability to provide enough warheads by subdivision of the available throw-weight. In that situation, even a very limited ABM deployment could make a major difference to the feasibility of such an attack.[54]

---

[51] Even more 'exotic' than a laser system is the distant possibility of a charged-particle-beam ballistic-missile destroyer. In recent months, Major-General George J. Keegan, Jr. (the retired head of USAF Intelligence) has stirred great controversy by claiming that the Soviet Union is on the brink of developing a weapon using such a technology. See Keegan, 'New Assessment Put on Soviet Threat', *Aviation Week and Space Technology*, Vol. 106, No. 13 (28 March 1977), pp. 38–48.

[52] For similar reasoning see Jan Lodal, 'Assuring Strategic Stability: An Alternative View', *Foreign Affairs*, Vol. 54, No. 3 (April 1976), p. 475.

[53] *Op. cit.* in note 13, Garwin proceeds to suggest that although his pebble-fan would work only against low-drag RV, high-drag RV would present attractive targets to automatic guns of the type currently being developed for low-level air defence.

[54] When *Safeguard* was appraised in the ABM debate of 1969, little or no account was taken of the fratricidal consequences of the radar-suppression wave of RV that many analysts fired hypothetically with confidence (or abandon). Also, one wonders why there has been no public discussion of the defensive value of deliberately-created fratricidal effects. Ballistic missiles launched and fired to explode so as to scatter destructive debris in the threat windows ahead of incoming missiles would be a high-confidence answer to theoretical hard-target counter-force dangers.

Super-Harden Silos

At a unit cost of nearly $1 million, the United States has now completed upgrading the blast resistance of the 550 *Minuteman* silos and their launch control centres (LCC) from 300 psi to 1,000 psi (there is one LCC to every flight of ten ICBM). These silos are also being hardened still further against electro-magnetic pulse (EMP) and radiation effects. But the blast resistance of missile silos is very difficult to estimate,[55] depending heavily on the features of terrain, just as missile accuracy may be degraded by unanticipated anomalies in the earth's gravitational field.[56] Despite the uncertainties, programmes have been proposed from time to time which would seek prolonged inviolability by means of physical protection. The hard-rock silo scheme of the United States, advanced in 1969, would have buried ICBM in silos blasted out of shock-attenuating stable terrain with a design resistance of close to 3000 psi (which approaches the compression tolerance of reinforced concrete). Consideration of cost and CEP trends dampened enthusiasm for this proposal: the total programmed cost was estimated to be no less than $5–6 billion, while predictable reductions in CEP would render the super-hard silos no less vulnerable than their predecessors.

By way of elementary (and simplified) illustration: if, in 1977, the SS-18 Mod 2 has 8 warheads of 2MT yield with CEP of 0·25 nm, it would have only a 0·345 probability of killing with one re-entry vehicle a silo hardened to resist 3,000 psi (with two warheads, cross-targeted, the probability is better than 0·60). If the CEP were halved to 0·125 nm, then the single-warhead version of an SS-18 would have a nominal kill probability of 0·82 and two cross-targeted warheads a probability of close to 0·99. Since the American MX ICBM should be capable of a CEP of 0·05 nm (304 ft) by the mid-1980s, it is not difficult to see why even those not greatly impressed with Soviet technological prowess are unwilling to endorse super-hardening. Moreover, American analysts have tended to assign the nominal psi resistance of American silos to most Soviet silos, and this is almost certainly inappropriate. The most recently upgraded Soviet silos are believed to have a psi resistance in excess of 2,000, and the great majority of Soviet silos are of more recent construction than their American counterparts. Moreover, the SS-17 and SS-18 ICBM, being cold-launched, are housed in silos with smaller, less vulnerable apertures than are hot-launched missiles.[57]

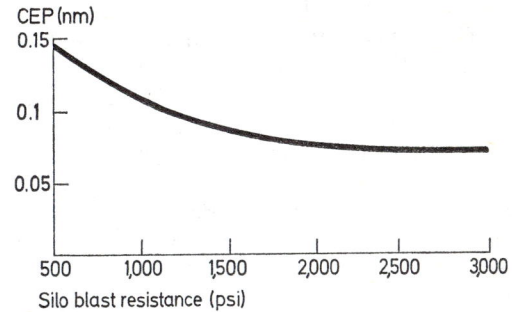

Figure 2: Silo Hardening

Task: To achieve a single-shot kill probability of 95 per cent with a 1MT warhead.

Source: Boeing 'Vulnerability Assessment Calculator'.

Figure 2 offers a graphic illustration of just how little extra resistance to blast can be purchased by silo-hardening: to offset an increase in the blast resistance of silos from 2,000 to 3,000 psi, one need improve missile CEP by only 60ft. Moreover, at 3,000 psi nuclear weapon effects other than blast would probably be of dominant concern. Since all-inertial guidance should eventually provide CEP of very nearly 0·05 nm (304ft), it is clear that silo super-hardening offers no worthwhile benefits to either super-power. Against a Soviet silo hardened to withstand 2,500 psi, a Mk 12A warhead (340KT) would need a CEP of 0·055ft to achieve a kill probability of 95 per cent. This is close to the asymptotic range for (non-terminal) all-inertial guidance, but the enormous cost of upgrading silos from 1,500 to 2,500 psi resistance would hardly be attractive, since it would burden an attacker with the need to improve his CEP by only 60 ft.[58]

---

[55] See Michael Nacht, 'The Vladivostok Accord and American Technological Options', *Survival*, May/June 1975, pp. 109–10.

[56] This is why defence analysts cite as a major source of uncertainty over ICBM CEP the fact that ICBM have never been tested over operational trajectories.

[57] See glossary, under 'cold launch'. MX, cold-launched by canister, *could* achieve a throw-weight as high as 15,800 lb and still be housed in *Minuteman* III silos (modified by the removal of internal shielding).

[58] In upgrading the silos for the SS-17/-18 series, it would seem that Soviet planners have ignored their systems analysts.

Silo super-hardening might begin to be cost-effective if it clearly required an attacker to move to terminal guidance and if terminal guidance was well beyond the present state of the art. Neither condition will be true for the 1980s.

Deploy Mini-ICBM in Silos
Stategic stability could be ensured if, rather than limiting the number of launchers, SALT permitted severely constrained ICBM payload to be distributed among a very large number of silo-housed ICBM (aiming points). With such a common ICBM payload ceiling (most unlikely to be achieved in SALT),[59] and sensible dispersion of that payload, neither super-power could pose plausible threats to the second-strike retaliatory capability of the other's land-based ICBM forces. Even if theoretically very great threats were posed, the fraction of mini-ICBM that should escape would still constitute a very large force. With the benefit of very advanced technology in the fields of nucleonics, guidance, fuel and metallurgy, a throw-weight allocation of, for example, two million pounds (or 1,000 *Minuteman* III at 2,000 lb each) could be transformed into a force of 10,000 mini-ICBM, each with a throw-weight of 200 lb.[60] Depending upon whether or not the warheads were designed to withstand the weapon effects of terminal defences, the yield of a mini-ICBM could be in the range 50–300KT. Presuming equal technical competence, both sides could be confident that in the face of large threats a high number of ICBM would survive. If each side could achieve a total kill probability of 90 per cent, the first-striker would disarm himself with his attack, leaving the adversary with 1,000 mini-ICBM out of a 10,000 ICBM force. The incentive to attack in such a context could not be high.

This scheme would meet any criterion of stability and would pose no problems for the monitoring of compliance with arms-control agreements. The predictable difficulties facing this 'option' are the need to induce Soviet acceptance of a common ceiling on ICBM payload, the need to persuade Western arms controllers that more strategic weapons are not necessarily undesirable in terms of the goals that they seek to attain, and cost. It is possible that very large-scale mini-ICBM deployment would be uncomfortably expensive. However, cost could be kept down by not investing in very expensive hard silos.

Finally, mini-ICBM deployment would offer lower vulnerability per warhead than would the high-payload ICBM of the MX variety. MX would place many warheads at risk to a single interception by boost and mid-course ABM systems.

Phase Out Silo-housed ICBM
Deploy Land-Mobile ICBM
Since the mid-1960s a series of official studies and reports have explored the cost and the technical and strategic operational feasibility of a very wide range of mobile-basing options, but thus far there has been no consensus on strategic need. This consensus is now gathering, as Donald Rumsfeld intimated.[61]

There are nine alternative land-mobile basing modes that merit identification: buried-trench mobility, dispersed-shelter mobility, garage mobility, off-road random crawling, road mobility, rail mobility, canal mobility, deep-pond mobility (connected by canals), and lake-bottom crawling.[62] Although each of these options is defensible, the first two would appear to present the least problems for the 'defender' without degradation in strategic effectiveness. (Problems can be solved, but only at a price.) Most of the more extensively mobile modes (off-road random, road, rail, canal, deep-pond/canal and possibly lake-bottom) entail the acceptance of potentially disturbing risks, would not be rigidly separable from civilian society, and pose problems for the adversary which could, in theory, be solved.

---

[59] The Soviet Union might become interested in severe payload reductions if such reductions were comprehensive in their coverage. To induce Soviet acceptance of a common payload ceiling, the United States could attempt to trade the payload of her long-range manned bomber force for Soviet ICBM payload.
[60] Paul Nitze has advocated a level of 5,000. See US Senate, Committee on Foreign Relations, *Warnke Nomination, Hearings*, 95th Cong., 1st sess. (Washington DC: USGPO, 1977), p. 140.
[61] *Op. cit.* in note 15, pp. 122, 130.
[62] See Edgar Ulsamer, 'M-X: The Missile System for the Year 2000', *Air Force Magazine*, Vol. 56, No. 3 (March 1973), pp. 41–2; 'USAF Pushes Advanced ICBM Studies', *Aviation Week and Space Technology*, Vol. 101, No. 2 (15 July 1974), pp. 100–1; John W. Hepfer, 'M-X and the Land-Based ICBM', *Astronautics and Aeronautics* (February 1975), pp. 57–61; 'B-1 Bomber Crux of SAC Plans', *Aviation Week and Space Technology*, Vol. 104, No. 19 (10 May 1976) pp. 43–5; and Lt-Gen. Alton, D. Slay, 'M-X, A New Dimension in Strategic Deterrence', *Air Force Magazine*, Vol. 59, No. 9 (September 1976), pp. 44–9.

BURIED-TRENCH MOBILITY

Deploying MX ICBM in buried trenches is the present leading contender in the debate on how this missile should be deployed.[63] The buried trench scheme would deploy almost 300 in concrete tunnels, probably 10 to 20 miles long, on the Yuma Gunnery Range in Arizona. (Alternatively, on grounds of cost, the tunnel could provide hardened concrete sections only at random, rather than a continuous concrete cylinder with uniform resistance to weapon effects.) The missile would (most likely) move on rails at random and could break out of the 'keystone' in the tunnel roof at any point. This concept could ensure pre-launch survivability and would not pose problems of CEP degradation, but the cost could be prohibitively high if the whole buried trench were constructed with ambitious blast resistance. A continuously hardened 'line' target, such as a buried trench, might be designed to provide protection up to 600 psi, but, the engineering problems it would involve are immense. In comparison with discrete hardened shelters connected by fairly soft roadways, the buried trench concept could be prohibitively expensive.[64] Moreover, the buried-trench scheme, as currently envisaged, is almost certain to draw very heavy criticism from environmental groups who will object to the digging of 3,000–6,000 miles of tunnels through the fragile ecology of the south-western desert.[65]

By way of added refinement, buried trenches could come to assume the proportions of 'buried trench complexes', a totally subterranean version of the garage complexes discussed below. However, in terms of cost (not to mention arms controllability) mobility with above-ground shelter connections would appear to offer superior deployment options.

CONTINUOUS MOBILITY: DISPERSED SHELTERS

A well-designed dispersed-shelter system would ensure survivability, combining deception with proliferation of aiming points. Missile transporters would move continuously, and at random, among a complex of hard (300–600 psi) shelters. For maximum deceptive effect transporters could deposit and pick up missiles within the shelters and carry dummy loads when they were not bearing missiles. Because the security of the missile depends on continuous deception, rather than the transporter 'dashing' for the silo at 60 mph or more, the roads linking the shelters need not be very expensive. The entire operation of this system could be masked from satellite, or even ground, sensors by shielding the roadways. Figure 3 illustrates the possible geometry of a dispersed-shelter mobile system.

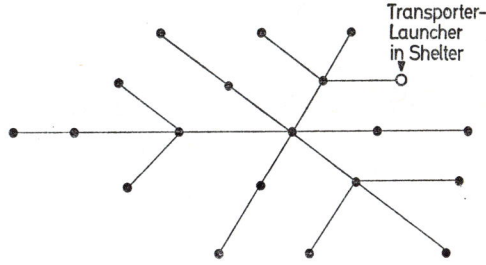

Figure 3: A Dispersed-shelter System

Hypothetically, a system comprising 300 land-mobile ICBM could offer 20 × 300 aiming points – which, if the conservative targeting rule of two warheads per shelter were adopted, would generate a requirement for 12,000 independently targetable re-entry vehicles and a force structure encompassing 400 complexes would require 16,000 re-entry vehicles. The cost of such a land-mobile system should be competitive with the B-1 and *Trident* I systems (in the $20–25 billion range) for threats of up to 10,000 re-entry vehicles. That judgment presumes shelter unit costs of $6–800,000. If shelter costs could be reduced to $2–400,000 each, threats on the scale of 20,000 re-entry vehicles could be defeated.

Unless it was saturated, there is no way in which this system could be defeated. But it is not certain that the cost-exchange ratio would be

---

[63] See Clarence A. Robinson, Jr., 'Minuteman Production Defended', *Aviation Week and Space Technology*, Vol. 104, No. 3 (19 January 1976), p. 14; and Slay, *op. cit.* in note 62, p. 47.

[64] Some officials familiar with the problem argue that new tunnelling technology should have a fairly dramatic favourable impact upon the likely costs of buried-trench mobility.

[65] Strategic calculation suggests that it is unwise: (*a*) to deploy MX as close to the sea as southern Arizona; and (*b*) to deploy it very close to the Mexican border. Ideally, MX would be deployed in the centre of the United States under working farmland (annual ploughing would damage or destroy any sensors a potential adversary might place over the tunnels).

[66] A useful brief description of this concept is 'B-1 Bomber Crux of SAC Plans', *op. cit* in note 62, pp. 42–5.

favourable to the defender. The throw-weight of the SS-17–19 series is so great that a programme of payload sub-division would enable a Soviet force of approximately 1,300 ICBM (to cite a low figure) to carry something like 30,000 200KT MIRV. The cost of the shelter system would be determined by the hardness selected: the higher the psi resistance of the individual shelters, the more expensive they would be. To achieve a single-shot kill probability of 95 per cent with a 200KT warhead against a shelter hardened to 300 psi requires a CEP of 608ft, against a shelter hardened to 600 psi the required CEP is 456ft. It would appear that high psi resistance, at great cost (increasing by up to four times), would be a flawed design concept: against a rapidly mounting scale of threat, and given the historic downward trend in CEP (see Figure 1), the security of a dispersed shelter system would have to depend upon the proliferation of modestly hardened shelters (300 psi).

Garage Dash Mobility

In a garage-mobile system, each ICBM is housed in a central 'garage', connected to 10–13 hardened launch sites or shelters (see Figure 4). On warning of attack, the ICBM (housed in a cold-launch canister) is moved at high speed to one of the launch sites, selected at random. The essence of this system comprises last-minute deception and the proliferation of aim points. A force of 1,000 ICBM would be transformed into a target system with up to 14,000 aim points,[67] and this number could be expanded considerably by adding shelters at appropriate intervals along the 'spokes' connecting the central garage to the shelters on the rim. This system, in common with the dispersed shelter option, would not provide shelters designed to withstand a very near miss, nor require elaborate and very expensive launch facilities at the potential launch sites: most of the missile-firing support systems would be carried with the missile on its transporter-launcher. In 1976, Malcolm Currie, the Director of Defense Research and Engineering in the US Defense Department, estimated that the acquisition of a land-mobile force of 300 MX ICBM would cost something like $15 billion in FY 1976 dollars.[68] It is reasonable to anticipate operating costs of roughly $5 billion over a ten-year period, making a grand total of $20 billion for acquisition and ten years of operation.

A garage-mobile system could be defeated by the provision of sufficient accurate MIRV to target each possible launch site. However, adequate growth potential could be ensured by providing

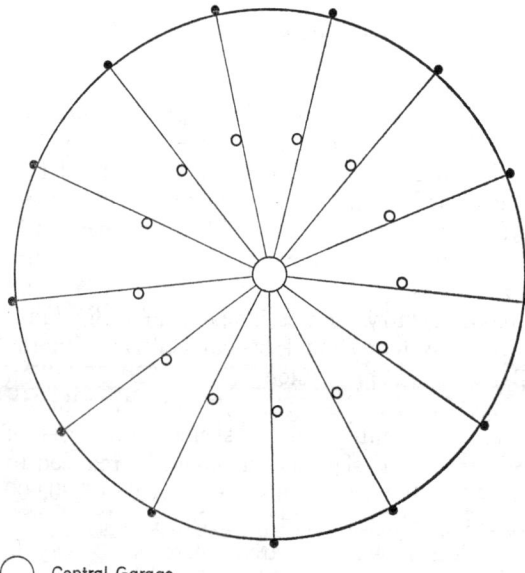

○ Central Garage
● Hardened Shelters/Launch Sites
o Secondary Hardened Shelters/Launch Sites

Figure 4: The Garage-mobile ICBM

[67] It is just conceivable that a post-boost vehicle could be informed, via satellite reconnaissance, which spokes of the target complexes were being used. But, given that the transporter-launcher might utilize several shelters *en route* to the shelter(s) at the rim, only very late real-time information would be adequate. Quite apart from the fact that navigational assistance of this kind would be difficult to design, to provide at tolerable cost, and to protect against interference or attack, it seems somewhat far-fetched to believe that low-drag re-entry vehicles would have enough time between re-entry and impact (20 to 30 seconds) to realign themselves accurately. This need not be a fatal flaw. Missile transporters might be committed irrevocably to a particular shelter several minutes before the re-entry of the incoming warheads. If manoeuvring high-drag PGRV did seem likely to pose a threat even to randomly-transported garage-mobile ICBM, the crude but effective solution would be to provide real-time reconnaissance-proof coverings to the spokes of the garage-shelter wheel (which would clearly violate any arms-control verification provisions modelled on Section 3 of Article XII of the ABM Treaty of SALT I).

[68] Testimony in US House of Representatives, Committee on Appropriations, Subcommittee on the Department of Defense, *Department of Defense Appropriations for 1977, Hearings*, Part 3, 94th Cong., 2nd sess. (Washington DC: USGPO, 1976), p. 97.

hardened shelters in such numbers that warhead proliferation on a massive scale would be required to saturate the system. For example, if each garage complex added a shelter on each spoke, a force of only 300 ICBM would offer a total of 8,100 aiming points, which should require the attention of 16,200 warheads for conservatively planned target coverage with insurance.[69]

In a detailed study, Desmond Ball and Edward Coleman have sought to demonstrate the technical feasibility of a garage-mobile system.[70] Its strategic and political attractions are obvious. This is not a system of continuous, nor near-continuous mobility, as envisaged above (and as would be required in some schemes for rail, road, off-road, and canal-mobility); hence, the risk of damage to sensitive instruments caused by the motion of the transporter should be minimal and the system's reliability should be very good. The required escape speed from the central garage could be estimated as a function of the warning time anticipated: indeed, for safe escape the transporter could be over-designed in terms of its attainable speed, so that a complex of spokes could be constructed long enough to allow eventual construction of a number of additional shelters along those spokes if needed. In short, this system has all the advantages of the silo-housed ICBM: separation from civilian society (its land requirements are substantial, but not forbidding), security, ease of command and control, and very high accuracy. Politically, a garage-mobile system meets any reasonable demand.

Among the limitations of the system is that growing cost could render shelter proliferation uneconomic if the adversary increased the number of RV for his offensive missiles, the high cost of the hard roads required for the high-speed dash, and the fact of the dash-dependence of the system. If a garage-mobile system of this character were purchased, two legs of the triad would be critically dependent upon very short warning time for survival (manned bombers and land-based ICBM). For the United States at least, a dash-dependent system would therefore be a poor instrument for the conduct of the strategic arms competition.

Finally, garage mobility falls foul of two major factors: one a conservative planning instinct, the other an arms-control perspective. Dash-dependent concepts have not, as yet, been eliminated from serious consideration for adoption in conjunction with an MX ICBM, but very few strategic planners would choose a deployment concept that required an instant response to tactical warning, if any reasonable alternative were on offer (for manned bombers there is no reasonable alternative).[71] The shell game notion described above, of continuous mobility between dispersed shelters, provides just such a reasonable alternative. The arms-control objection to garage mobility is the same as to dispersed-shelter mobility: it could be very difficult, short of comprehensive on-site inspection, to know just how many ICBM the complexes house.

On balance, the garage-mobile ICBM deployment concept must be judged inferior to the buried-trench and dispersed-shelter notions discussed above. All land-mobile concepts will be very expensive (for example, the operation and maintenance of one silo-housed ICBM requires approximately eight men: a mobile ICBM would probably need 40–50)[72] in comparison with continued silo-basing. It would therefore make little sense to adopt a deployment mode which contained a major vulnerability: real-time detection of the transporter dash. Also – and this applies to buried trenches, dispersed shelters and dashing garage mobiles – the cost-exchange ratio of shelters to MIRV could well move markedly against shelters (and their associated linking roadways and operation and maintenance costs). The proliferation of hard, or even semi-hard,

---

[69] The 8,100 aiming points are produced by 300 complexes, each with 13 shelters around the 'rim', 13 on the 'spokes', and 1 central garage. (See Fig. 4). Even if the Soviet SIOP did not plan to devote two warheads to each shelter and garage, this deployment scheme – providing it has no Achilles' heel – does require a massive scale of attack. The Soviet Union's calculations might indicate that the garage complexes could be given saturation coverage, but she should anticipate that prospects for a restrained American response, after an 8,100–16,200-RV attack on the American homeland, could not be promising.

[70] 'The Tootle Solution: An Analysis of a Land-Mobile ICBM System', unpublished paper (July 1975). For a revised and shortened version, see *Survival*, July/August 1977, pp. 155–163.

[71] Strategic Air Command has consistently declined to construct hard shelters for its aircraft, despite some analyses indicating their value. For a classic analysis of the value of shelters, see A. J. Wohlstetter, F. S. Hoffman and H. S. Rowen, *Protecting US Power to Strike Back in the 1950s and 1960s* (Santa Monica, Cal: Rand Corporation, R-290, 1 September 1956).

[72] 'B-1 Bomber Crux of SAC Plans', *op. cit.* in note 62, p. 45.

shelters provides no certain cost-effective solution to the hard-target counter-force threat. It is quite possible that land-mobile shelter concepts, like traditional-type ABM systems, will be overtaken over the next decade by the scale of the deployable threat.

OFF-ROAD RANDOM CRAWLING

Off-road random crawling systems could face major navigational, security and politico-strategic problems. A true countryside-roamer, even if it is an air-cushion vehicle, must increase the out-of-service time of an ICBM (suspension in a silo is very different from carriage over the deserts of the south-western United States). Canister-housing should ensure temperature control, general protection from the environment and some protection against nuclear-weapon effects, but the problems of technical reliability could be serious. The reduction in accuracy could be offset by NAVstar assistance and precision guidance. A good solution to the problem of CEP degradation would be to have the off-road crawlers circulating at random among very dispersed shelters, or – relying heavily upon the hardness of the canister – among pre-designated launch points.

Surface crawlers, even when moving in a random fashion, would be visible to a variety of potential enemies. ICBM might be targets for dissident groups, and it is difficult to see how command and control could be rendered invulnerable to nuclear effects, considering the random movements of the transporter.[73] Even if (as one must presume) such a system were mobile only on military preserves, physical protection and communication would present problems of the utmost gravity. More to the point perhaps, even if the problems had actually been solved, a random-roaming system could hardly fail to make politicians and officials anxious. Missiles in canisters should be safe against most nuclear-weapon effects other than blast from near misses, but a very substantial fraction of a land-mobile ICBM force might be disabled fatally were it caught in the open, between well-dispersed shelters, by a 'barrage' attack of high-yield weapons. Also, the fact that the cloudier parts of the United States lack the kind and extent of terrain appropriate to a random-crawling system would help Soviet reconnaissance and navigation satellites to provide up-dated target information. Cost estimates for an off-road mobile system vary in the range of $12–15 billion to $30–50 billion (for research, development and procurement over an eight to ten year period).[74]

ROAD AND RAIL MOBILITY

Road- and rail-mobile systems would probably entail trying to hide ICBM among civilian traffic patterns. Even on little-used road and rail networks, these systems would be vulnerable to other than strategic disruptions. Both strikes on the railways and weather conditions could reduce the free-ranging potential of these weapons. Furthermore, road- and rail-mobile ICBM would be relatively accessible to hostile groups.

In principle, the Soviet Union should be more attracted to off-road, road- and rail-mobile ICBM basing concepts than the United States, given her far greater territory and the character of her political life. However, she would face equal problems of system reliability, and possibly tenuous command and control.

Off-road mobility could entail traversing some very rough country in both the United States and the Soviet Union, where the climate is far from temperate, while road and rail mobility would be restricted, in the less-populated sections, by less than extensive networks of roads and tracks. A convincing case for off-road, road- or rail-mobile ICBM basing has yet to be advanced.[75]

CANAL/DEEP-POND MOBILITY

Canal and deep-pond/canal mobile basing modes also suffer from several debilitating limitations. Briefly, canal traffic is slow-moving (compared with road or rail traffic), and canal networks, in the United States at least, are in profound disrepair. Admittedly, ICBM would be very difficult to target if sited on the bottom of deep pools (a

---

[73] It is occasionally argued that the real vulnerability of the *silo-housed* ICBM force is in the area of command and control.

[74] For the cost estimates, see Paul H. Nitze, 'Assuring Strategic Stability in an Era of Detente', *Foreign Affairs*, Vol. 54, No. 2 (January 1976), p. 229; and Lodal, *op. cit.* in note 52, pp. 474–5. Nitze's range of $12–15 billion was in 1975 dollars.

[75] The operational feasibility of rail mobility is probably very high. With some ingenuity, a large number of ICBM could be concealed among regular civilian rail traffic. Clearly the option to avoid would be the organization of special 'missile trains', the movements of which could easily be monitored by an enemy on a real-time basis.

depth of 40ft has been cited),[76] provided an enemy did not know which pools contained missiles, but the procession of large missile barges to and from such sanctuaries could hardly be kept secret from reconnaissance satellites, secret agents or (in the United States) groups who are sentimental about canals. No doubt the physical security of missile barges could be guaranteed, but the cost and anxiety involved seem to be prohibitive.

There is, however, at least one variant of the deep-pond concept which merits serious attention. A complex of ponds could be excavated and connected with fairly soft roadways for slow-speed missile transporters. The ponds would serve as the functional equivalents of the semi-hard shelters in the dispersed-shelter and garage systems discussed earlier (a deep pond could offer a psi resistance of almost 600 and might cost around $150–200,000), but, in contrast to the above-ground 'drive in, drive out' shelters, ICBM would launch from the ponds. In terms of physical security, deep-pond complexes on military reserves pose no greater (or lesser) problems than do any above-ground shelter systems. There is no indication of substantial official interest in this deployment mode at present, which is surprising in view of the relative costs of using ponds as opposed to shelters (and certainly to covered and concrete-hardened trenches).[77]

LAKE-BOTTOM MOBILITY
Finally, ICBM could be transported on the backs of lake-bottom crawling vehicles. The problems of command and control over vehicles on the bottoms of fresh-water lakes would be minimal in comparison with the difficulties of communicating through salt water to very distant SSBN,[78] but they would still be far more substantial than for silo-housed ICBM, or buried-trench mobile, dispersed-shelter or garage-mobile ICBM. In northerly latitudes ice coverage would present a problem for many months of the year, though this could be solved. If the vehicles crawled at random among a set of pre-selected and marked launch sites on lake bottoms, the problems of CEP degradation as a consequence of mobility should be precluded. Lake-bottom crawlers or submerging missile barges would pose serious engineering problems and would require costly protection from the environment but should be invulnerable; they would be difficult to seize; their CEP should be excellent; and they should enjoy acceptably reliable real-time communication with command authorities. However, they would most probably prove prohibitively costly compared with dispersed shelter and garage-mobile concepts. American officials have dismissed lake-bottom mobility because of the anticipated public hostility.

Deploy Air-Mobile ICBM
For several years the United States Air Force has been advocating air-mobile ICBM as a partial answer to the problems posed by the impending vulnerability of silo-housed missiles.[79] Air-mobility would be very expensive, however. Apart from the cost of the missiles, a fleet of carrier-aircraft would have to be developed (or converted or redesigned) and procured. Boeing believes that an MC-747 (a 'straightforward derivative' of the 747F already in service) could accommodate four ICBM weighing 100,000 lb each, or eight ICBM of 50,000 lb (*Minuteman* III has a launch weight of 76,000 lb; MX could weigh as much as 172,000 lb).[80] To deploy a force of only 200 MX could therefore require no less than 100 wide-bodied jets (at a 'fly-away' cost of some $35–40 million each).

The principal difficulties to be overcome before an air-mobile option would be a serious contender for adoption are cost-effectiveness, CEP degradation and vulnerability. The cost argu-

---

[76] 'USAF Pushes Advanced ICBM Studies', *op. cit.* in note 62 p. 101. In this article the pools are to be connected by a road network (which would offer considerable advantages in terms of speed of movement compared with a canal network).

[77] As an engineering task, it would be difficult to specify anything simpler than the digging of a hole, lining it, providing a ramp, and constructing connecting roadways. But underwater storage, (some) maintenance, and launch would pose too many engineering problems of such magnitude that they would not be tackled, given the availability of attractive alternatives.

[78] See Edgar Ulsamer, 'Survivable Command and Control – A Military Imperative', *Air Force Magazine*, Vol. 58, No. 7 (July 1975), pp. 70–1.

[79] In March 1973, the Senior Editor of *Air Force Magazine* went so far as to write: 'Although most of the experts concerned with future strategic systems now favour air-mobility, the land-mobile concept has not been abandoned'. (Ulsamer, *op. cit.* in note 62, p. 41).

[80] Edgar Ulsamer, 'Adjusting Triad to Mounting Soviet Threats', *Air Force Magazine*, Vol. 57, No. 4 (April 1974), p. 55.

ment promises to be decisive, because air-mobile ICBM could hardly fail to be the most expensive means of delivering warheads (not excluding the SSBN force) in a context where other survivable options would be available. There is a CEP degradation problem inherent in release from an aircraft, free fall by parachute, attitude alignment and mid-air ignition, but, while it will be difficult to ensure that air-launched ICBM attain CEP not inferior to those of land-based ICBM, missile navigation is progressing so rapidly that success should be anticipated.[81]

Vulnerability presents a more serious problem. As James Schlesinger observed, 'the aircraft with the missile aboard could be kept on ground alert, but then it would have the same pre-launch vulnerabilities as the bomber/tanker force'.[82] A study by Boeing has explored three air-mobile operational modes: standby, dispersed ground alert, and airborne alert. On standby alert, aircraft would require approximately two hours for transition to full alert status. On dispersed ground alert, assuming an efficient early-warning system for detecting SLBM launches and basing deep in the interior of the American continent, the aircraft should require an escape time of four minutes (and this figure could be reduced). On airborne alert, aircraft could be kept aloft for periods varying between twenty-two and seventy-two hours, with air-refuelling every ten hours. Boeing's basic assumption has been the need to ensure the survivability of 200 air-mobile ICBM. To maintain twenty-five aircraft on airborne alert (with eight 50,000 lb ICBM to a carrier) would require a fleet of thirty-six carrier-aircraft and twelve tankers.[83] The operation and maintenance costs of an airborne alert would be dramatically higher than the costs of any variant of ground alert status.

Provided a super-power was willing to pay for a protracted and dispersed ground alert (aircraft fuelled, crews on board, or in trailers on the runway, missiles loaded and immediate access to runways ensured), the survivability of an air-mobile ICBM force should pose no very grave problems. However, the costs of this basing mode would be so high that it is very unlikely to be adopted.[84]

Deploy Air- or Sea-launched Cruise Missiles
Cruise missiles may be considered to offer three alternatives for the strategic posture. First, they could be deployed as the second leg of a dyad (replacing ICBM *and* manned bombers), on aircraft designed or converted for optimal performance as cruise-missile carriers. Second, they could be deployed as a third, semi-independent, leg of a triad, in conjunction with SSBN and a penetrating bomber force, but with missions not confined to supporting bomber penetration. Third, and as the Carter Administration may choose, cruise missiles could be deployed as a means both of prolonging the life of older manned bombers, and of improving the prospects for penetrating bombers (cruise missiles could help saturate and suppress enemy defences, as well as strike directly at urban-industrial and military target systems).

The attractions of long-range cruise missiles (LRCM) have been well advertised. They include low procurement cost ($500–750,000 – excluding the warhead – compared with $10 million for an ICBM);[85] small size and launch weight; very high

---

[81] NAVSTAR satellites would provide navigational fixes to within 20–30 feet for the carrier aircraft and the 'dropped' ICBM, or stellar navigation aids could be employed, while an AIRS system would be married to a PBV and to re-entry vehicles fitted with a range of precision guidance technologies – e.g. a passive microwave radiometric correlator, an active radar range/cross section correlation device, and a terrain contour matching (TERCOM) system for elevation profile matching.

[82] *Op. cit.*, in note 17, p. II-28. This is not strictly true. Wide-bodied jets, benefiting from an as yet technically unproved rocket-assisted take-off, could not climb out of danger (SLBM launch) as fast as B-1 bombers. Also, because of their size and construction details, they would be more vulnerable to nuclear effects than custom-built bombers.

[83] *Op. cit.*, in note 80, p. 56.

[84] See Cecil Brownlow, 'DoD Leans to Land-Based MX', *Aviation Week and Space Technology*, Vol. 102, No. 7 (17 February 1975), pp. 14–15.

[85] The exact fly-away cost of a cruise missile cannot be predicted at present, because of uncertainties over the size of the production run and the scope of the conversion required to fit ALCM into B-52 (and possibly B-1) weapon bays. A baseline figure for ALCM deployment is 1,000. That number could be accommodated on 50 of the 255 B-52G/H. To fit into SRAM dispensers, the range of ALCM would be restricted to approximately 650 nm. The total cost of the cruise missile programme could be very high indeed if one had to take account of the purchase of a fleet of special carrier aircraft. A specific unit cost estimate for the ALCM is $620,000 (*excluding* research and development and nuclear warhead costs). See General Jones' testimony in *op. cit.* in note 68, p. 136. When research and development costs are added, the unit cost of an LRCM will rise to close to $1.2 million. The Air Force/

accuracy (as air-breathing vehicles they are powered and guided throughout the flight); and operational options that pose major problems for the defence (for example, penetration at 60–300ft, amidst the 'ground clutter' that blinds existing Soviet downward-looking airborne radars[86] and a very low radar cross-section). Moreover, the above features create a total capability greater than the sum of its parts: relatively low cost means that the deployment flexibility inherent in the small size and weight can be fully exploited. Housed in rotary racks, on pylon mounts or in converted bomb bays, air-launched cruise missiles (ALCM) could add 650–1,300 nm to the reach of the carrier aircraft. Housed in weapon bays specifically designed to accommodate them, ALCM could attain any range likely to be useful strategically, and an aircraft fitted with ALCM need not penetrate terminal defences. Sea-launched cruise missiles (SLCM), housed in the standard torpedo tubes of submarines and surface vessels (or indeed on a wide variety of mountings), could, in principle, give hunter-killer submarines or even destroyer types a strategic role.[87]

On the negative side, cruise missiles pose major arms-control problems;[88] their pre-launch invulnerability can be no better than that of their carrier-vehicles; their subsonic speed (the second generation should acquire a supersonic 'dash' capability) means that they are slow to target and in principle liable to interdiction by sophisticated air defences; and they would lack the operational flexibility of the penetrating bomber.[89] Leaving aside the particular Soviet-American disagreements of 1975–77 over the status of LRCM that have hindered progress towards a SALT II treaty, it is the flexibility of this family of technologies (which flows, essentially, from the small size of the missiles) that creates arms-control difficulties. Cruise missiles may be deployed in all environments except outer space (being air-breathing vehicles), and their precision-guidance navigational aids permit the fitting of nuclear or conventional warheads, as preferred. It is almost certain that LRCM will be deployed for both tactical and strategic missions, while their multi-purpose technical character and their ease of varied deployment must greatly hamper any attempt to count them for strategic or theatre arms limitation agreements.[90]

ALCM, probably fitted with warheads of around 200KT, and guided by terrain contour matching (TERCOM) technology and its successors,[91] should be capable of striking at any hard target. (Indeed, because of their more flexible guidance systems, ALCM should perform better than any ballistic system, however navigated, against a land-mobile target system.)[92] However, in the absence of terminal ABM defences, cruise missiles would face operational problems far graver than those confronting ballistic systems: their carrier aircraft might suffer severe attrition on the ground and *en route* to their weapon release points. Moreover, the Soviet air defences of the late 1980s will not be permissive. One should anticipate a major Soviet effort to develop low altitude

---

Boeing ACM-86A has a range of 650 nm, but the ACM-86B, the 'stretched' version, will have a range of 1,300 nm. See 'USAF Pushes Long-Range Cruise Missile Version', *Aviation Week and Space Technology*, Vol. 106, No. 16 (18 April 1977), pp. 19–20.

[86] The American AWACS has solved this problem – one should presume that the Soviet Union could deploy a fair facsimile of a mid-1970s American AWACS by the mid- to late 1980s.

[87] For the technical and probable strategic-operational characteristics of LRCM, see Kosta Tsipis: 'The Long-Range Cruise Missile', *Scientific American*, Vol. 233, No. 1 (July 1975) pp. 15–26, and 'Cruise Missiles', *op. cit.* in note 13; for a dramatically contrasting view, see Robert L. Pfaltzgraff Jr and Jacquelyn K. Davis, *The Cruise Missile: Bargaining Chip or Defense Bargain?* (Cambridge, Mass.: Institute for Foreign Policy Analysis, January 1977).

[88] See Richard Burt, 'The Cruise Missile and Arms Control', *Survival*, Vol. XVIII, No. 1 (January/February 1976), pp. 10–17; and Alexander R. Vershbow, 'The Cruise Missile: The End of Arms Control?' *Foreign Affairs*, Vol. 55, No. 1 (October 1976), pp. 133–46. For a very different point of view see Colin S. Gray, *Who's Afraid of the Cruise Missile?* (Croton, NY: Hudson Institute, HI-2511-DP, September 1976).

[89] Unlike manned penetrating bombers, cruise missiles will not sense the operation of (mobile) SAM radars and hence (attempt to) fly around the air defence hazard.

[90] Any SALT agreement which placed restrictions on the range or character of warheads of cruise missiles would be quite unverifiable. This is not the equivalent of claiming that cruise missiles cannot be accommodated in an arms-control regime. See Tsipis, *op. cit.* in note 13, p. 29.

[91] A useful detailed description and discussion is presented in Tsipis, *op. cit.* in note 87 and *op. cit.* in note 13. Also very useful is 'Air-launched Cruise Missile Flight Nears', *Aviation Week and Space Technology*, Vol. 106, No. 8 (23 February 1976), pp. 67–9.

[92] However, precision-guided manoeuvrable re-entry vehicles on ICBM or SLBM would, in their terminal phase, behave as cruise missiles (with or without active thrust in that phase).

surface-to-air missiles which are mobile (and hence incapable of advance suppression), an airborne warning and central system and a new generation of long-range interceptors capable of looking down and shooting down – overcoming the short-comings of current Soviet airborne radars.[93]

The attractiveness of strategically targeted ALCM and SLCM should depend, to a large extent, upon the decision taken on the future of land-based ICBM. If a high-confidence land-based ICBM should be purchased, the need for a large force of ALCM would not be obvious, and the performance required of the airborne leg of the triad should be lower. ALCM and SLCM would not be completely satisfactory as a direct substitute for land-based ICBM, since the range of the current generation of LRCM would still be short (relative to ICBM and SLBM), they would be slow to target, and both they and their carrier vehicles could suffer defensive counter-force attrition.

Strategic Choice: Images of Power and Deterrent Effect

The attractiveness of the complex choices outlined above must depend upon doctrinal preferences and upon judgments concerning the relationship between appraisals of the super-power strategic-weapons balance and perceptions of what may be termed the will to exert political influence.

Strategic dyads are defensible, analytically, for both super-powers, but they would have unattractive operational limitations. In his article in *Foreign Affairs* in January 1973, Fred Iklé suggested that the United States need not require all her strategic forces to be ready for instant use.[94] This is interesting in that one could conceive of the United States and her allies spending so much (and so wisely) on local defences that the strategic forces would have no plausible mission beyond the deterrence of strategic use on the part of the Soviet Union. However, some substantial fraction of American strategic forces needs to be ready to intervene very rapidly in the event of a local conflict developing catastrophically. One cannot predict just how quickly an American president might wish to prosecute some limited strategic options, or to attack Soviet ICBM held in reserve after a limited hard-target counter-force first strike by the Soviet Union, but having a survivable land-based missile force available, would provide certainty of a responsive military instrument to hand.[95] In the words of Dr Malcolm Currie, the former American Director of Defense Research and Engineering: 'I would say that we will want to maintain our land-based ICBM capability at its maximum numbers as long as we can because they provide the only very rapid response capability that we have. They are a very accurate force, a very highly controllable force against time-urgent targets, and we have all too little of that capability already.'[96]

Which mobile alternative to the silo is the most cost-effective? Every basing mode has theoretical vulnerabilities, if only the crude one of susceptibility to a saturation attack. Every system that provides multiple aiming points is open to the criticism that it might be cheaper for the adversary to augment his RV than for the defence to build shelters and connecting roads. Of the land-mobile possibilities, the shell-game of dispersed shelters and the buried-trench option would seem to be the most interesting.

Since there are no cheap, simple and rapidly deployable alternatives to the silo-housed ICBM force, it is perfectly appropriate for officials and analysts to ask just how desirable a triad may be compared with a dyad (of much smaller overall dimensions), and whether the theoretical risks of a dyad are not acceptable. However, one cannot contemplate the future of land-based missile forces without being aware that the answers given to underlying (and possibly unresolvable) questions tend to shape the results of the analysis. These are: just how important is the perceived

---

[93] American advocates of major LRCM deployment tend to be undismayed by the prospective enhancement of Soviet air defence capabilities. One recent American study estimates that 'the Soviet Union, to counter current generation low-flying, pre-programmed, highly accurate cruise missiles targeted against Soviet territory, would be forced to spend between an estimated $10 and $15 billion for the modernization of its air defence system'. Pfaltzgraff and Davis, *op. cit.* in note 87, p. 10.
[94] Fred Iklé, 'Can Nuclear Deterrence Last Out the Century?', *Foreign Affairs*, Vol. 51, No. 2 (January 1973), p. 283.
[95] There is no way of knowing from unclassified sources how great the time penalty might be of depending upon SSBN for LSO. If SSBN trail antennae on or very near the surface, there is, of course, no time penalty. However, SSBN can be lost that way.
[96] *Op. cit.* in note 68, p. 97.

state of the strategic balance (and to whom), and how is the strategic balance perceived by those with the political authority to act upon their perceptions?

Compared with perceptions of relative economic performance and relative influence in regions of common interest, how would a strategic stand-off between a dyad and a triad weigh in the perception of the overall balance? One could argue that the world is becoming ever more complex, and that – particularly when neither side can plausibly threaten to *win* an intercontinental war – crude comparisons of the super-power strategic-weapons balance mean very little for the freedom of foreign-policy action perceived by each side. Indeed, if the United States were to decide against all land-based deployment options for missile forces, it is possible that senior Soviet officials might begin seriously to question the wisdom of maintaining their own land-based missile forces (particularly if American officials were to advertise vigorously a CEP of 200ft or so for *Trident* II SLBM). However, Soviet officials might also perceive (or misperceive) a relative weakening in American strategic prowess and come to believe that the United States would lack the immediate strategic options that her triad had provided. Each super-power should prudently seek to avoid those visible disparities in military strength that might be interpreted abroad as a sign of weakness, but it cannot be demonstrated that particular dangers would be certain to flow from perceptions of those disparities.

The strategic arms race has not been one of blindly competitive behaviour on both sides. Today, as over the past decade, the Soviet Union deploys fewer than 200 dedicated long-range bombers, and therefore has less of a triad than has the United States.[97] However, this does not suggest either a Soviet disdain for questions of strategic appearances, or that an American dyad (of SSBN and manned bombers) would fulfil all necessary political functions *vis-à-vis* the Soviet triad. Since the 1950s the Soviet Union has invested in those strategic systems which should yield the greatest political returns. The 'missile gap' in the Soviet favour predicted for the early 1960s was not a myth: it was fulfilled at the level of medium- and intermediate-range ballistic missiles relevant to the discouragement of NATO Europe.[98]

Yet, it is probably a mistake to attempt to isolate the question of appearances designed for perceptual effect when appraising the evolution of the Soviet strategic posture. As may be easily illustrated by referring to authoritative Soviet statements, military power is viewed, comprehensively, within a framework of political purpose.[99] Considerations of appearances mesh constructively with war-fighting (and hence, in the Soviet view, deterrent) requirements. Observers of the various East–West military balances are, presumably, impressed not only (or not so much) by static measures of strategic capability as by indices of political determination – and also by what those indices, translated into dynamic measures, would most probably mean in the event of crisis and war.

The main argument against the United States moving unilaterally to a dyad comprising SSBN and manned bombers or cruise missile carriers is

---

[97] Careful analyses of the bomber legs of the super-powers' triads are distinguished by their absence. If one refrains from assessing 'airmindedness' in terms of two-way *intercontinental* mission capabilities, the Soviet Union emerges with the largest dedicated bomber force in the world. Careful analysis in the West of Soviet air power is exceedingly rare, but the B-1/cruise missile issue has begun to stimulate some impressive analysis of American strategic air power. By far the most persuasive assessment of B-1 related issues is Francis P. Hoeber, *Slow to Take Offense: Bombers, Cruise Missiles, and Prudent Deterrence* (Washington DC: Center for Strategic and International Studies, Georgetown University, February 1977).

[98] For useful, recent comment, bearing particularly upon the impending modernization of this force with the MIRV SS-X-20, see Richard Burt, 'The SS-20 and the Eurostrategic Balance', *The World Today*, Vol 33, No. 2 (February 1977), pp. 43–51.

[99] In September 1975, Andrei Gromyko, the Soviet Foreign Minister, wrote in *Kommunist*: 'The predominence of the forces of peace and progress – a predominance which has now grown appreciably – gives them the opportunity to determine the channel followed by international politics. ... As a whole the activity of the Warsaw Pact organization exerts a great positive influence on the shaping of the situation not only in Europe but far beyond its borders' ('Peace Program in Action', translated in FBIS *Daily Report*, USSR National Affairs, 22 October 1975, p. R16). On a similar theme: 'The more powerful our Motherland becomes, the more opportunities it acquires for influencing the course of world events in a direction favourable to the peoples'' (V. Korionov, 'Solidarity Is the Source of Strength of the Peoples', *Pravda*, 23 July 1972). Many such examples could be given. What is impressive is that *every* careful study by Western scholars of Soviet understanding of the relationship between military power (latent force) and political influence reaches the same broad conclusion: Soviet officials consider them to be intimately related.

geopolitical. The United States needs to project credible military power across the North Atlantic and North Pacific in opposition to a potential enemy that enjoys a growing local predominance in conventional and theatre-nuclear striking power.[100] Confronting the Soviet triad, as currently and predictably configured, strategic nuclear intervention by an American dyad would probably be both incredible and liable to fail if exercised. Current American and NATO strategy presumes that limited strategic options provide additional deterrence to NATO's theatre defences. But LSO, to be credible and politically effective, require a strategic capability in reserve to dissuade a coercive reply that would probably prove politically persuasive.

Two claims are being advanced here. First, that an American dyad facing a Soviet triad, would convey an image of relative lack of political determination. Second, that an American dyad would indeed offer strategic options inferior to those provided to Soviet leaders by their triad. The United States needs to persuade sceptical Soviet and allied officials (and indeed herself) that American strategic nuclear forces would be fired *first* in the event of local catastrophe in Europe. Unilateral abandonment of land-based missile forces could hardly fail to contribute to a weakening both of American political resolution over strategic-nuclear first use and of allied and Soviet perceptions of the likelihood of such use.

V. SOME ARMS-CONTROL CONSIDERATIONS

Because of her strategic doctrine, and because of the political advantages (both unilateral and offsetting) that her leaders believe to be likely to flow from it, it is extremely improbable that the Soviet Union would sign a SALT agreement which would effectively preclude the vulnerability of American ICBM silos. With the Soviet Union at present in the process of deploying three (and possibly four) MIRV-equipped ICBM systems and with a successor series under development, an arms-control solution to the problem of coping with the future survivability of land-based missile forces is unlikely unless the United States invests heavily in a dedicated hard-target kill capability (essentially in MX) that should motivate Soviet leaders to seek alternatives to silo basing.

The potential contribution of a radical SALT III to strategic stability is easy to identify but would be very difficult to accomplish. Officials on both sides should be able to appreciate that they face a common problem in the obsolescence of silo-housed ICBM, and consequently should devise arms-control schemes which prevent the threat to silos from developing or provide for the phasing out of silo-housed ICBM to a common timetable. Unfortunately, strategic forces are instruments of political competition and have not – thus far, at least – lent themselves to Western arms-control criteria of arms race and crisis stability.[101] A serious joint attempt should be made to see if the common problem can be resolved in concert (tacitly or formally), although it would not be surprising if such an effort failed. Arms-control analysis and planning in the West continues to reflect Soviet thought in ways which could be misleading.[102] It is possible that Soviet officials do not believe that political instability must result from technical strategic instability. Even if they were to accept that the vulnerability of silos was a common problem, it is very far from certain that they would favour radical arms-control schemes requiring a restructuring of *their* strategic forces.

If the United States were to move towards the more interesting options discussed above to

---

[100] See US Senate, Committee on Armed Services, *NATO and the New Soviet Threat*, Report by Senators Sam Nunn and Dewey F. Bartlett, 95th Cong., 1st sess. (Washington DC: USGPO 24 January 1977); and Joseph D. Douglass, Jr., *The Soviet Theater Nuclear Offensive* (Washington DC: USGPO, 1976).

[101] The ABM Treaty of 1972 constitutes a major exception to this rule. The growing debate over the threat to silo-housed ICBM in the 1980s seems to suggest that the technical stability criteria that drove American SALT negotiators in the early 1970s were inadequate. Throughout the SALT I negotiations, the formal American position was that ABM constraints *must* be tied to restrictions upon hard-target killing potential. As early as 1973-74 it was evident, even to those commentators who favoured SALT I, that that condition had not been secured.

[102] See Colin S. Gray, 'Detente, Arms Control and Strategy: Perspectives on SALT', *The American Political Science Review*, Vol. LXX, No. 4 (December 1976), pp. 1242-56.

alleviate the vulnerability of land-based missiles, serious difficulties would be created for arms-control negotiations. Terminal defence of missile silos would require the rewriting of the ABM Treaty of 1972, while most of the land-mobile possibilities would place intolerable strain upon national technical means of verification. American officials might be compelled to choose between a SALT III regime that cannot be adequately verified and the demise of the SALT system. It would be difficult, though not impossible, to render dispersed shelters, garage-mobility and covered trenches compatible with the kind of verification that the American defence community and public opinion deems essential, but it is difficult to say just how relaxed the Soviet defence community would feel about American land-mobile systems. If the SALT system is perceived not so much as a vital adjunct to strategic force structure, but rather as an interdicting set of political requirements, then it may be felt necessary to pay some strategic price of possible consequence in order to maintain the health of the SALT system. Specifically, despite the many arguments for retaining land-based missiles, American leaders could elect to move to a dyad. This decision could be implemented preferably by explicit agreement, but unilaterally if necessary.[103]

It seems sensible to argue that the super-powers should seize the historical opportunity for a major reduction in strategic armaments that must arise from the vulnerability of silos. Could they not make a virtue of necessity and agree, in the context of SALT III, to reduce progressively the Vladivostok ceiling of 2,400 delivery vehicles (to, for example, 2,000, 1,750, 1,500 and below) – or, much better, agree to descending constraints on payload, with no constraints on numbers – with the mutual understanding that the reduction would be effected principally in the ICBM legs of the triads? The bilateral phasing out of ICBM forces would be admirable as a measure of disarmament, but its contribution to international security would be more problematical. The removal of ICBM forces would have an ambiguous effect upon the survival prospects of SSBN and manned bombers. Command of the SSBN fleets is threatened mainly by ICBM, while removal of American ICBM should greatly enhance the effectiveness of Soviet air defences. SSBN and manned bombers might be menaced convincingly by SLBM launched on depressed trajectories, by ASW forces and by active air defences.

With weapon technology advancing very rapidly, and political rivalry between the super-powers unlikely to abate markedly, it would be dangerous to place a high value upon the securing of SALT agreements *per se*. Arms-race and crisis stability depend upon the mutual retention of large, diverse and flexibly-optioned strategic forces. SALT agreements which greatly simplify the attack-planning problems of one, or even both, sides should be avoided. Without transition to a land-mobile leg of the triad, massive reductions in the silo-housed ICBM forces, whether or not accompanied by augmentation of the SSBN and bomber fleets, would make little contribution to stability, however defined. The path to the serious alleviation of strategic problems does not lie primarily through East–West arms-control negotiations. If short-term radical reductions in the threat to hard-targets are not negotiable, and longer-term phased bilateral movements towards dyadic postures cannot be secured through formal agreement, then strategic policies may have to be pursued which run counter to conventional arms-control thinking.

None of the options presented above for responding to the predicted vulnerability of missile silos poses arms-control problems of such severity that it should be disregarded for that reason alone. Launch-on-warning should worry an adversary, but declarations of such a tactic are worth considering seriously only in a situation that is already deemed desperate. Terminal ABM defences are theoretically innocent in terms of arms-control; indeed, to the extent that they might preclude the need for new and very expensive basing modes, they may even be attractive to arms controllers. (Unfortunately, however, they require the rewriting of the most solid

---

[103] As should be clear from the argument in the preceding sections of this study, I would be very strongly opposed to the United States taking such unilateral action. However, Western arms-control theory might just lead an American President in this direction. To preserve a SALT system which was believed to generate valuable political spin-off, apart from its function as the centre-piece of detente structures, the United States might well (*a*) endorse a SALT II or III regime which would guarantee the near-term (theoretical) vulnerability of ICBM silos, and (*b*) evacuate her silos, without parallel land-mobile deployment, because suitably robust 'counting rules' for land-mobile ICBM could not be devised.

accomplishment achieved in SALT so far.) If arms controllers are interested in stability, then they should consider a combination of land-mobile ICBM basing and terminal ABM defence.

Air-mobile ICBM would pose only the most elementary of counting problems. The existence of SLCM and ALCM could destroy confidence in the observance of specified limits of offensive force levels, but one should enquire just what might be gained even by a large-scale surreptitious deployment of these weapons. With ballistic missiles benefiting dramatically in accuracy from AIRS, NAVstar, stellar navigation and PGRV, long-range cruise missiles offer 'more of the same' (only more slowly delivered). They could not strike targets immune to advanced ICBM.

In their classic study, *Strategy and Arms Control*, Schelling and Halperin wrote: 'Adjustments in military postures and doctrines that induce reciprocal adjustments by a potential opponent can be of mutual benefit if they reduce the danger of a war that neither side wants, or contain its violence, or otherwise serve the security of the nation. This is what we mean by arms control.'[104] If arms control cannot accomplish Schelling and Halperin's aspirations, one should at least ensure that it does not hinder them. On arms-control grounds it is sensible to be cautious, though not dismissive, about land-mobile systems and long-range cruise missiles, but – if the SALT process shows no signs of alleviating strategic problems through co-operative endeavours – one should also be wary of vulnerable silos and manned bombers and cruise missiles that would have great difficulty in penetrating to their targets. Given the specific operational limitations of SSBN and bombers, the super-powers should maintain land-based missile forces, provided cost-effective deployment solutions can be found to the threat posed by an increasing payload subdivision which is more than offset by the reduction in missile CEP.

This study advances two claims. First, despite the apparent paradox, a serious SALT III agreement will be possible only if the United States invests convincingly in a dedicated hard-target killing MX follow-on ICBM, deployed in a survivable mode. The scale of Soviet investment in silo-housed ICBM and upgraded silos is such that nothing less than a credible threat to their second-strike integrity would lead to their evacuation. Persuasion in SALT is a matter of bargaining leverage, not *per se* of the substance of arguments (on the putative dangers of crisis instability and so forth). The second claim is that land-mobile ICBM are not inherently impervious to national technical means of verification within tolerable uncertainties.

VI. CONCLUSION

It is tempting to stand back from the technical detail of strategic weaponry and ingenious scenarios and ask, 'so what?'

It has been suggested above that silo-housed ICBM should be phased out and replaced by a land-mobile system, almost certainly of greatly reduced proportions. It has also been argued that, through the 1980s and beyond, both super-powers, separately or jointly, would be best served by a triadic structure. The salient questions, addressed in part by such authors as Walter Slocombe, Edward Luttwak and Uri Ra'anan,[105] are: what would be the political consequences of one party to the arms race (*a*) permitting its rival to acquire a strategic inventory that appeared to be far more *substantial* than its own, and (*b*) permitting its rival to acquire a strategically far more *capable* inventory of weapons? Some might not be convinced that a theoretical imbalance in hard-target counter-force capability would have any notably disadvantageous political consequences. After all, even if either (or both) super-powers' silos were to prove as vulnerable as pre-

---

[104] Thomas Schelling and Morton Halperin, *Strategy and Arms Control* (New York: Twentieth Century Fund, 1961), p. 143.
[105] Walter Slocombe, *The Political Implications of Strategic Parity*, Adelphi Paper No. 77 (London: IISS, May 1971); Edward Luttwak, *The US–USSR Nuclear Weapons Balance*, The Washington Papers, Vol. II, No. 13 (Beverly Hills, Cal.: Sage, 1974), and *op. cit.* in note 3, Part I; Uri Ra'anan, US Senate, Committee on Government Operations, Subcommittee on National Security and International Operations, *International Negotiation, The Changing American–Soviet Strategic Balance: Some Political Implications*, Memorandum, 92nd Cong., 2nd sess. (Washington DC: USGPO, 10 March 1972).

dicted by careful strategic analysis, a first striker would still be accepting the most severe of risks in seeking to disarm an ICBM force while of necessity leaving many SSBN and bombers free to roam at large. Intra-war deterrence might work, but it might very well not – and our historical data on its functioning in the context of nuclear use is precisely nil.

It is difficult, though necessary, to relate strategic weapons to possible foreign policy choices. This study has assumed that choices made with respect to strategic posture should be of international political importance. But, as Bernard Brodie has suggested, in the minds of most people thermonuclear war between the super-powers is really 'the impossible war'.[106] To worry about the political consequences of possible strategic imbalances, one need not predict inimical behaviour from abroad. The claim that ICBM silos will be vulnerable and that a land-mobile system is probably the most cost-effective and necessary successor does not imply that the first super-power to attain an almost total disarming capability against silos would be inclined to foment crises and indulge in a partial first strike against them. The details of hypothetical super-power crises in the late 1980s are, to say the least, obscure. However, as James Schlesinger has written: 'Deterrence ... is not something free-floating that exists independently of a credible implementable threat. It requires the most careful structuring of forces that is fully consistent with an agreed upon strategic concept.'[107] To advocate a land-mobile basing mode for American and Soviet ICBM for the mid- to late 1980s is not to presume that the adversary is necessarily likely to exploit a context of vulnerable silos. It is simply a claim that airborne weapon carriers and SSBN have particular operational weaknesses, and that it would be unwise to offer such a large, even provocatively tempting, target system as vulnerable ICBM forces for his first-strike attention.

Superiority in strategic appearances and unmatched Soviet strategic options might have no consequences in terms of Soviet strategic behaviour, being but one factor among many influencing Soviet assessments of the correlation of forces between the super-powers. However, strategic nuclear forces are perceived very widely as the *ultima ratio* of a super-power, and their perceived importance has been demonstrated both in the scale of the Soviet strategic build-up of the past decade and in the rhetorical prominence attached to the outcome of SALT. Neither super-power is likely to move unilaterally to a strategic dyad, and, though a triad containing land-mobile ICBM might seem over-designed for plausible threats, the consequences of major errors of strategic choice could be so final that some over-design is wise.

---

[106] Bernard Brodie, *War and Politics* (New York: Macmillan, 1973), pp. 416–32.

[107] *Op. cit.* in note 17, p. 1–11.

APPENDIX

The principal authorities for this Appendix were the IISS annual *The Military Balance, Jane's Weapon Systems* (annual), *Aviation Week and Space Technology* (weekly) and *Air Force Magazine* (monthly). The details offered are the sole responsibility of the author.

I: Strategic Missiles

Category[1] and type	Max. range (000 statute miles)[2]	Throw-weight (000 lb)[3]	Warhead yield	CEP (nm)[4]	First deployed	No. deployed (July 1977)
The United States						
ICBM						
Titan II	6·3	8	9MT	0·5[5]	1962	54
Minuteman II	6+	1	1–2MT	0·3	1966	450[6]
Minuteman III	7+	2	3 × 170KT (MIRV)[7]	≤0·15[8]	1970	550
MX[9]	8	8–10[10]	13 × 340KT (MIRV)[11]	≤0·05[12]	(Probable IOC 1986)[13]	
SLBM						
Polaris A3	2·88	1	3 × 200KT (MRV)	0·5	1964	160
Poseidon C3	2·88	2–3	10 × 50KT (MIRV)[14]	0·3	1971	496
Trident I (C4)[15]	4·6	3+	8 × 100KT (MIRV)[16]	0·2–0·3[17]	(Planned IOC, 1979)[18]	
Trident II (D5)[19]	7·5	5+	7 × 340KT (MIRV)[20] / 14 × 150KT (MIRV)[20]	0·115[21]	(Planned IOC, 1987)	
LRCM						
ACM 86 A/B ALCM / Tomahawk SLCM	[22] 0·75–1·5[23]	0·2–0·3	≥200KT[24]	0·005–0·016[25]		
The Soviet Union						
ICBM						
SS-7 *Saddler*	6·9	3–4	5MT	1·5	1961	109[26]
SS-8 *Sasin*	6·9	3–4	5MT	1·0	1963	
SS-9 *Scarp*						
Mods 1, 2	7·5	12–15	18–25MT	0·5	1965	238[28]
Mod 4			3 × 5MT (MRV)[27]			
SS-11 *Sego*						
Mod 1	6·5	1·5	1–2MT	0·5	1966	840[31]
Mod 3[29]		2	3 × 100–300KT (MRV)	0·3–0·4[30]	1973	
SS-13 *Savage*	5	1	1MT	0·7	1968	60[32]
SS-X-16	5+	2	n.a.[33]	0·25–0·3[34]		
SS-17						
Mod 1	6·3+	6	4 × 900KT (MIRV)[35]	0·3	1975	40
Mod 2			5 MT?[36]			

32

Category[1] and type	Max. range (000 statute miles)[2]	Throw-weight (000 lb)[3]	Warhead yield	CFP (nm)[4]	First deployed	No. deployed (July 1977)
SS-18						
Mod 1	6·3+	16–20	18–25MT	0·25–0·34	1974	50+
Mod 2			8 × 2MT + (MIRV)[37]		1976	
Mod 3			10–15MT?	0·2–0·25	1977	
SS-19						
Mod 1	7+	7	6 × 1–2MT (MIRV)	0·25–0·34	1975	140
Mod 2	6·3+		5MT+	0·2–0·25		
SS-?[38]	n.a.	n.a.	n.a.	n.a.		
IRBM						
SS-5 *Skean*	2·3	1	1MT	1·5	1961	100
SS-20[39]	3·5–4·6[40]	n.a.	3 × 150KT + (MIRV)	n.a.	1977	
MRBM						
SS-4 *Sandal*	1·2	1	1 MT; or HE	1·0	1959	500
SLBM						
SS-N-5 *Serb*	0·75	1·5	1–2MT	1·0–2·0	1964	{ 24 on SSBN[41] 30 on SSB }
SS-N-6 *Sawfly*						
Mods 1, 2	1·75	1·5	1–2MT	1·0[42]	1969	544
Mod 3	2		2–3 × KT(MRV)			
SS-N-8	4·85[43]	2–3	1–2MT	0·5[44]	1972	232
SS-NX-17[45]	3+	3+	1MT	0·2–0·3		
SS-NX-18[46]	5+	5+	3 × 1–2MT (MIRV)			

[1] ICBM range = 4,000 statute miles, IRBM = 1,500–4,000, MRBM = 500–1,500, LRCM = over 350.

[2] Range and payload are traded off against each other.

[3] 'Order of magnitude' estimates. Throw-weight is the weight of payload (weapon(s)) and guidance equipment deliverable over a stated range in a particular trajectory. If maximum range is desired, payload must be diminished.

[4] As may be seen from the standard counter-force formula, $K = Yield^{2/3}/CEP^2$, CEP is the most critical of all values in counter-force formulae (except at very low levels indeed, with large weapon yields). Yet it is the one about which least is known with confidence. Neither super-power issues authoritative CEP estimates for its own or the other's missiles. The figures here are the best estimates obtainable from a very imperfect public record.

[5] The *Titan* II guidance system is so obsolescent that the USAF is facing servicing difficulties. Retrofitting the *Minuteman* III (or the *Titan* III space booster) guidance system into *Titan* II is being considered, which would both solve servicing problems and greatly reduce CEP. *Titan* II has been retained in the SAC inventory because of its contribution to the throw-weight sub-balance.

[6] There are no plans (publicly announced at least) to phase out *Minuteman* II. The Command Data Buffer System, which permits retargeting in 25 minutes, is not being installed for reprogramming *Minuteman* II.

[7] Mk 12 re-entry vehicles. The 340KT Mk 12A should be retrofitted by 1980–81.

[8] An early 1976 figure offered by Lodal, 'Assuring Strategic Stability: An Alternative View', *Foreign Affairs*, Vol. 54, No. 3 (April 1976), p. 465. Improvements in the existing guidance system (the NS-20) are expected to reduce CEP to better than 0·1 nm.

[9] At present, common technological building blocks are being designed so that MX could be silo-housed, land-mobile or air-mobile (air launching and some land-mobile modes would require different guidance technologies). MX would fit into *Minuteman* silos.

[10] This range may be pessimistic, depending upon progress in the development of new high-energy rocket propellants. Since MX is only at the threshold of engineering development, no authoritative figures are available.

[11] These are the Mk 12As which are to be retrofitted on to *Minuteman* III. Rather than proliferate the Mk 12A, it may be decided to deploy the result of the Large Ballistic Re-entry Vehicle (LABRV) development (formerly known as the Mk 20) with a yield in the MT range, or to proceed to a precision-guided manoeuvrable re-entry vehicle.

[12] This estimate presumes that MX will employ AIRS and a new-generation on-board computer. If AIRS functions as

anticipated (first flight tests in 1976 were satisfactory), there will be no clear case for proceeding to a PGRV. At such a low CEP hard-target counterforce success will depend on (a) the ability to increase missile and warhead reliability by cross-targeting, and offset expected unreliability by launching second warheads, and (b) the design of re-entry vehicle tactics to overcome fratricide phenomena. These phenomena probably preclude the tactic of rapid re-programming that was analytically popular several years ago (see footnote 3 to text).

[13] IOC= initial operating capability. The date of 1983 was reasonably authoritative for the Ford Administration in late 1976; under President Carter, 1985 is probably a better estimate.

[14] The *Poseidon* C3 SLBM is variously credited with a payload ranging from 6 to 14 RV (10 being most commonly cited as a median figure). The critical determinant of payload is the range required (in conjunction with the character and number of aiming points).

[15] The US Navy plans to purchase 576 *Trident* I SLBM at a cost of $6·6 billion: 240 for 10 *Trident* SSBN, 160 to retrofit 10 *Poseidon* SSBN (scheduled for FYS 1980–4), and 176 for testing and spares.

[16] Mk 4 RV. The (MARV) Mk 500 *Evader* could be carried but its evasive capability seems redundant in the absence of any but token ABM defences.

[17] The principal strategic advantage conferred by *Trident* I over *Poseidon* is the extra sea-room that it permits the SSBN with the great extension of SLBM range. Moreover, because of the employment of a new stellar inertial guidance system, there is a small reduction in CEP. However, with Mk 4 RV yields of only 100KT, *Trident* I has no future as a silo-killer.

[18] *Trident* I is to be retrofitted onto 10 *Poseidon* SSBN. The *Trident* submarine construction programme is being funded, year-by-year, on a 1-2-1 basis. (The lead submarine was funded in FY 1974 – hence the tenth submarine will be funded in the request for FY 1980.)

[19] Unlike *Trident* I, *Trident* II will only fit into the launch tubes on *Trident* submarines. Critics of *Trident* II have suggested that the US Navy set its design parameters so that a new class of SSBN would have to be built to deploy it. The USAF has, apparently, declined to endorse a common technology programme for MX/*Trident* II, on the grounds that the constraints of a *Trident* SSBN's launch tubes reduce throw-weight too much.

[20] These options are illustrations of the kind of payloads *Trident* II could carry but are not predictions. It is possible (and, if MX is not pursued, almost certain) that *Trident* II will carry PGRV for maximum hard-target counter-force effect.

[21] This estimate seems not unreasonable for a stellar inertial guidance system, aided by progress in the software of precise navigation, in the late 1980s. AIRS could halve this in theory, but, comprising a sealed sphere, is not compatible with stellar inertial navigation (required to compensate for SSBN navigational error).

[22] Essentially, common technology programmes. Major design constraints are that the *Tomahawk* SLCM must be capable of launching from a standard torpedo tube and from a B-52, while the Boeing ALCM has been designed for compatibility with SRAM racks and avionics. The shorter-range ALCM under construction (ACM 86A), is 14ft long, the SLCM 20·5ft. See *Aviation Week and Space Technology*, Vol. 104, No. 22 (31 May 1976), p. 11; J. Philip Geddes 'The Sea Launched Cruise Missile', *International Defense Review*, 2 (1976), pp. 198–202; Pfaltzgraff and Davis, *op. cit.* in text note 87.

[23] As of 1977 the *Tomahawk* SLCM could have twice the 750-mile range of the ACM 86A ALCM. With respect to attacking targets deep in the Soviet Union the latter is not truly a stand-off weapon. The only distinction that lends itself unambiguously to clear verification is between short-range tactical and long-range strategic cruise missiles. The former should be powered by turbo jet engines, the latter by turbofans – each has a very distinctive infra-red signature. See Tsipis, *op. cit.* in text note 13.

[24] It has been announced that strategic cruise missiles would have the same warhead yield as SRAM (200 KT).

[25] Presumes the application of terminal guidance technology: specifically the TERCOM system, preferably with the assistance of NAVstar.

[26] Withdrawing SS-7 and SS-8 from the active inventory, and dismantling their facilities, has begun. Under the Protocol to the Interim Agreement of SALT I, the SS-7 and 8 ('ballistic missiles of older types deployed prior to 1964') may be replaced by an equal number of SLBM (up to a total of SLBM 'on submarines' of 950). Delay in dismantling SS-7 and SS-8 as four *Delta* II SSBN went to sea led to a leaked charge of a SALT I violation. See 'Newest Delta Sub Pivotal in Latest SALT Violation', *Aviation Week and Space Technology*, Vol. 104, No. 21 (24 May 1976), pp. 20–1.

[27] SS-9 has been identified in four Mods: Mod 1, with an 18MT RV; Mod 2, with a 25MT RV (the bulk of the diminishing total of SS-9 deployed); Mod 3, with a single RV (tested 1967-71 in FOBS and depressed-trajectory modes but not known to be operational); Mod 4 with three multi-MT MRV (commonly presumed to be 5MT each). Mod 4 has served also as a test vehicle for the MIRV programmes.

[28] Reduced from a maximum of 288. The SS-9 is being replaced by the SS-18. The Soviet Union's 'heavy ICBM' allocation of 303 under SALT I, which will be carried over into SALT II, will hardly be wasted on the SS-9 now that the MIRV-capable SS-18 is available.

[29] SS-11 Mod 3, a very successful 3-MRV development tested from 1969 to 1973, requires slight modification to silos built for SS-11 Mod 1. This has helped to frustrate Henry Kissinger's 1974 aspiration that one of the least ambiguous criteria for identifying MIRV launcher deployment would be deployment in a modified silo.

[30] May be on the optimistic side. However, SS-11 Mod 3 is known to be more accurate than Mod 1.

[31] Includes 100 deployed in the IRBM/MRBM fields. The number should drop markedly over the next five years as SS-17 and SS-19 are phased in.

[32] SS-13 is expected to be replaced by the SS-X-16, which may be deployed in a mobile mode.

[33] The SS-X-16 is reported to have been tested only with a single RV. However, it is fitted with a PBV, which indicates very active interest in a MIRV option. It would be reasonable to expect it to carry three KT-range RV.

[34] CEP estimates for SS-X-16 must be even more uncertain than is usual for Soviet strategic systems, because of the strong possibility that it will be deployed in a mobile (and probably, though not certainly, CEP-degrading) mode.

[35] In 1974 James Schlesinger referred to MT-range war-

eads in the context of full deployment of SS-17 and -19; see also Robert L. Pfaltzgraff and Jacquelin K. Davis, *SALT II: Promise or Precipice* (Washington DC: Center for Advanced International Studies, University of Miami, 1976), p. 5.

[36] Tests of an SS-17 (Mod. 2) began in February 1976.

[37] The United States has insisted that all SS-18 deployed must be counted against the 1,320 MIRV launcher ceiling in SALT II. 'National technical means of verification' could not distinguish between MIRV and single-warhead versions.

[38] There is a new generation of Soviet ICBM that could be deployed early in the 1980s.

[39] SS-20 is intended as a successor to the obsolescent SS-4 and SS-5; but see Clarence A. Robinson, Jr., 'Another SALT Violation Spotted', *Aviation Week and Space Technology*, Vol. 104, No. 22 (31 May 1976), pp. 12–14; also Richard Burt, 'The SS-20 and the Eurostrategic Balance', *The World Today*, Vol. 33, No. 2 (February 1977), pp. 43–51.

[40] SS-20 essentially comprises the first two stages of the SS-X-16 ICBM. It has been tested extensively with 3 MIRV at the lower end of the range estimates, and with one RV at the higher end. If, as Western officials expect, SS-20 is deployed in large numbers (1,000+), the Soviet Union would have a force which could be upgraded to ICBM range – either by using a single RV or by adding the third stage of the SS-X-16.

[41] The 24 are aboard 8 *Hotel*-class SSBN, the 30 aboard 10 *Golf* II-class diesel-powered submarines. Because of ambiguities in the language of the Protocol to the Interim Agreement of SALT I, and in that of an 'agreed clarification' of 24 July 1974, it was unclear whether all, some, or none of the SS-N-5 were included in the SLBM ceilings. The eventual agreement, dated 3 July 1974, indicated that (a) SLBM on *Hotel*-class boats were included, and (b) SLBM currently deployed on *Golf* II-class boats were not included (but if they were replaced in a modernization programme, the new SLBM would be included).

[42] Probably on the high side for the Mods 2 and 3, both of which attained their IOC only in 1974. The SS-N-6 is deployed aboard 34 *Yankee*-class SSBN.

[43] SS-N-8 constitutes a major technical surprise in the arms race. The initial maximum-range estimate by Western intelligence circles was only 3,000 miles.

[44] May be on the conservative side, since SS-N-8 uses stellar inertial navigation for mid-course correction.

[45] SS-NX-17 is the first Soviet solid-propellant SLBM, and the first to be tested with a PBV. The values ascribed to this and the SS-NX-18 are very uncertain. SS-NX-17 is expected to replace some of the SS-N-6 on the *Yankee*-class SSBN.

[46] SS-NX-18 is the first Soviet SLBM to be tested with 3 MIRV. It is expected eventually to replace some or all of the SS-N-8 on board *Delta* I- and II-class SSBN. In addition, it will probably be carried abroad the forthcoming Soviet 24-tube SSBN.

II: Strategic Bombers

Category[1] and type	Max. range (000 statute miles)[2]	Max. speed (Mach no.)	Max. weapons load (000 lb)	Armament[3]	First deployed	No. deployed (July 1977)
The United States						
Long-range						
B-52D	9	0·95	60	4 × MT[4]	1956 ⎤	
B-52G	10	0·95	75	⎰ 8 SRAM and	1959 ⎬	373
B-52H	12·5	0·95	75	⎱ 4 × MT[5]	1959 ⎦	
Medium-range						
FB-111A	3·8	2·5	37·5	2 SRAM[6]	1969	68
The Soviet Union						
Long-range						
Tu-95 *Bear*	8	0·78	40	1 *Kangaroo*[7] ASM or 1–2 × MT	1956	105[8]
Mya-4 *Bison*	6	0·87	20	2 × MT	1956	35
Backfire B[9]	5	2·5	>20	*Kitchen* or ASM-6[10] ASM and 1–2 × MT	1974	85[11]
Medium-range						
Tu-16 *Badger*	4	0·8	20	1 MT	1955	750

[1] Long-range = 6,000 statute miles; medium-range = 3,500–6,000 miles, primarily designed for bombing missions.

[2] Theoretical maximum range, with internal fuel only, at optimum altitude and speed.

[3] Plausible standard force loadings, not the theoretical maximum.

[4] The Mk 28 1 MT bomb or the B-61 variable-yield (all under 1 MT) bomb, or some mix of the two.

[5] It is difficult to specify 'standard' armaments for B-52G/H. All have been modified to enable them to carry a *Hound Dog* air-to-surface missile (ASM) on a hard-point pylon under each wing, while some have been, and are being, modified to enable them to carry up to 20 SRAM (12 in 3-round rotary dispensers under the wings and 8 in a dispenser in the aft bomb bay). Alternatively, they could carry up to 20 ALCM. In addition, 4 Mk 28 and/or B-61 can be carried. A B-52G/H with 20 SRAM and 4 Mk 28 would probably be fortunate to stagger into the air, let alone penetrate Soviet air defences at low level.

Hound Dog has a speed of Mach 2·0 and a range of 600 miles, with a 1 MT warhead, while SRAM can attain Mach 2·5 and has a range of 35 miles (low altitude) to 100 miles (high altitude) with a 200 KT warhead.

[6] It is usual to specify 6 SRAM, but this requires four of them to be externally mounted, which drastically affects the aircraft's range and handling.

[7] *Kangaroo* has a speed of Mach 2·0, a range of 400 miles, and probably at least a 2 MT warhead.

[8] While all 105 could be used as long-range bombers, many of them function as maritime patrol and reconnaisance aircraft.

[9] *Backfire* B defies unambiguous categorization. With in-flight refuelling it is an intercontinental bomber, but it is most suitably configured for peripheral strike-reconnaissance missions around Eurasia.

[10] *Kitchen* has a range of 460 miles. ASM-6 is a new stand-off weapon, believed to have been designed for *Backfire* and reported to have a range of 490 miles and a speed of Mach 3·0.

[11] Total *Backfire* procurement must depend, in good part, upon the outcome of the SALT II negotiations. The 1977 production rate is reported to be 2 per month, and aircraft seem to be allocated fairly evenly between Long-Range Aviation and Naval Aviation. If the production rate continues for the duration of the projected SALT II regime, by late 1985 the Soviet Union will deploy close to 300 *Backfires*, perhaps 150 of them assigned to Long-Range Aviation.

It may be worth noting that for the first time in many years the American defence community is seriously considering the possibility that the Soviet Union might be 'working on the follow-on heavy bomber with greater range and payload to replace the aging *Bears* and *Bisons*'. See Donald H. Rumsfeld, *Annual Defense Report Department, FY 1978* (Washington DC: US Government Printing Office, 17 January 1977), p. 63.